Hard, but Good

A Spiritual Exploration of Suffering

By Emily Benjamin

This title is also available in Kindle format.

ISBN: 979-8-9881398-9-8

Cover design by Benj Mori.
Published with help from 100X Publishing. www.100Xpublishing.com

DEDICATION

This book is dedicated to every person who has ever taken up the call to cleanse their family bloodline and break generational curses. Don't give up. Don't turn back. There will be freedom in the end.

CONTENTS

Forgiveness and Greater Understanding

FOREWORD

By Magnus Sund

When I first met Emily years ago, I thought to myself, *this woman is on the brink of psychosis*. What I didn't know at that point was the horror, trauma, and pain she had experienced. I later discovered an upbringing that could have come straight from a horror movie. What I also didn't know was her internal power, strength, and resilience. Emily is remarkable, a true powerhouse. Not only is she doing an excellent job raising four children on her own and she is street smart and intelligent, but even more so, she has chosen to embrace love, life, and the truth when anything else would have been the easier option. Emily refused to remain in her trauma and let it define her. She refused to be a victim.

Emily's book arises from her experiences of pain, suffering, and horror. It is not a book that offers a philosophical perspective on suffering created from behind a safe desk. Instead, it emerges from the trenches of pain and horror. She did not shy away from the hard questions; rather, she ran toward them. How can God be good and not only allow suffering in the grand scheme, but how could He permit so much suffering in my own life? Wrestling with God like Jacob of old, she came out on the other side with a new name.

When you meet Emily in person or through her book, you don't encounter a victim or a slave. Instead, you meet a warrior, though not in a traditional sense. This is a tender, quiet, and patient warrior—someone who has walked through hell and emerged on the other side. Her unwavering commitment to finding healing, truth, and love is remarkable. If you want to read a book by a survivor of abuse and violence who refused to be a victim, offering her perspective on suffering, this is the book for you. It is truly a privilege to have gotten to know Emily and to call her a friend. I believe you will find her journey, as she describes in her book, life-giving, challenging, and healing.

My Story

CHAPTER 1

For the Lord gives wisdom;
from his mouth come knowledge and understanding.

—Proverbs 2:6

This is not the first book written on suffering, nor, I'm sure, will it be the last. My own understanding of the concept of suffering has been greatly influenced by the work and experience of others. One of the most important books I've ever read on the subject was *The Problem of Pain* by C.S. Lewis, in which he succinctly dispels the notion that we have a right to entertain atheism or accusations against God's character as a method of coping with our own experiences of pain and difficulty. I would highly recommend this book to anyone looking for further understanding of the unindictable character of God in the face of human suffering.

However, over the course of several years of intense healing, growth, and encounter with God, I have come to believe that I may have something of value to contribute to the discussion on suffering. I hope my perspective will result in others having, not just a greater understanding of the One who created them, but real, deep, and life-transforming encounter with that same Creator.

Various branches of the Christian church and theological schools of thought have come up with strikingly different points of view on the topic of human suffering across the centuries, and it can sometimes feel difficult to know what to believe. For example, monks once thought there was some great spiritual benefit to be gained through self-flagellation, often scourging themselves with whips in the hope of achieving great rewards in eternity. Then, on the extreme opposite end of the Christian spectrum are some modern theological perspectives, particularly in the Charismatic stream, so forcibly preaching the work of God's healing (which is true, and real, and absolutely essential to the abundant life offered to us through Christ) that they have often glossed over the very real, excruciatingly painful healing and restoration process that many people must complete in order to even be capable of receiving His promised abundant life. I hope to land at neither of these extremes, but at a place where God has revealed Himself to me in a tremendously tangible, life-altering way.

I must acknowledge before continuing that this book is primarily about revelation and understanding I have gained on the topic through my own suffering and through my journey of healing from it. As such, the histories and circumstances I will convey here will focus on these aspects. I do not in any way intend to claim a status of victimhood that relieves me of any responsibility I have had in the suffering of others. There are numerous individuals, a list's worth, to whom I know I have been the unfortunate vehicle of pain and suffering. The majority of these unfortunate circumstances are the product of my own brokenness and subsequent inability to navigate relationships and difficulties with any semblance of health, rather than the product of a desire to cause harm to others. In my broken state of desiring love, I have often not loved others well, though I had the desire to do so. I could likely write a book equally as long as this one about those individuals and circumstances, but it would not be very uplifting or enlightening. The catalyst for my own ability to love others in a healthy way was found in the healing of my own pain and trauma. Therefore, this book will detail the experiences that brought me to a place that I believe will result in my hurting far fewer people than in previous eras of my life.

This book is also not meant as a how-to guide for healing, although I do discuss it to some degree. There are many books already on that subject, written by individuals much more versed and trained in the process than myself.

Ultimately, this book is intended to be a conceptualization of the experience of human suffering, why it occurs, and how to view it in a way that leads to living victoriously rather than in victimhood, nearer to God rather than further from Him.

To accomplish this goal, I will first need to detail, to some degree, an overview of the suffering I have experienced throughout the course of my life. This background information will be necessary to fully grasp and appreciate the value of the understanding of suffering that I've subsequently gained during my own healing process and spiritual journey with the Lord.

CHAPTER 2

The Lord is close to the brokenhearted
and saves those who are crushed in spirit.

—Psalm 34:18

I grew up in the toxic theology that claims that God creates (or allows us to experience) specific instances of suffering so that we learn lessons—a perspective that would, as Bill Johnson has often stated, surely result in his arrest for child abuse if He was a human parent. And we would all agree with that arrest (unless we are psychopaths). I also grew up in a church deeply entrenched in punishment theology, often using verses such as, "God disciplines those he loves" (Heb. 12:6) to convince people that their sicknesses, relational problems, abuse, car troubles, financial setbacks, and every other form of difficulty faced in life were, or at least could be, God's way of disciplining them. *They just didn't follow Him well enough.* This, I was told, meant that He "loved" me.

And so, I grew up believing that every painful thing I had ever experienced was my own fault because I just didn't do well enough in trying to follow God's rules. When I tell you some of the painful experiences I had in early life, you will understand why this belief was so damaging for me personally. To some degree, it is always damaging for those who believe such things about a Father who in reality loves them deeply and grieves with them in their sorrow. But I have found that the greater damage in such theology is done to those who have suffered to a greater extent, because, you see, in this belief system, the amount of pain and difficulty you experience is the direct result of how well or how poorly you are following God. So, if you have suffered greatly, then you must be a worse person than most others and in need of greater "discipline."

I will try to explain why this theology had such ruinous effects in my own life.

I am the second oldest child of what turned out to be a very large family. I have been told numerous times in my life that my family should have had our own reality TV show. Thankfully, I was spared at least that trauma.

My father was and still is a pastor. He founded a church a few months after I was born. So, for the entirety of my formative years, my father was leading an Evangelical church congregation. Now, any of you reading this who are pastor's kids (PKs) will know that even under what we might consider "normal" circumstances, being a pastor's kid has its challenges—from people in the congregation believing that it's their right and duty to correct you (or inform on you to your parents) for everything they deem to be a mistake in your life, to what I have always thought of as the very odd existence of deep jealousy and hatred from peers who see you as somehow having a "privileged" PK status. I can assure you that the "position" of pastor's kid is not generally considered a positive experience by those who have grown up in it. I would have happily traded places with any one of my peers.

My father was also, unfortunately, a narcissist, it appeared. I do not mean this in the pop-culture sense of the word, which generally is meant to communicate that the person is prideful and thinks highly of themselves. My father *was* prideful and *did* think highly of himself, but anyone who has done in-depth research into the topic of narcissistic abuse will understand what is meant by narcissism in the truest sense of the word. Actually, it refers to a clinically diagnosable condition known as narcissistic personality disorder. Now, my father has never been diagnosed with this disorder by a psychologist. That would have involved him believing there was any reason for him to be assessed by a psychologist or that a psychologist might know more about the human mind than he did himself. However, I can tell you that I did not come to this conclusion about my father lightly. Though I have a degree in psychology, I have never been a licensed counselor or practiced psychology in a professional setting. However, having done a great deal of in-depth research into the topic of narcissism and narcissistic abuse, and even to this day, continuing to try to stay up to date on the newest research published on the subject, I feel very confident in my assessment of my father. He appears to easily meet the diagnostic criteria as it now stands.

Please do not misunderstand. I love my father. In fact, through the process of my own healing, which I will discuss later in this book, I came to have a depth of love for my father that I did not know was possible. My greatest prayer for him up to the time of the writing of this book is that he will know true freedom and healing, not so that I can have a restored relationship with him (though I would be happy with that outcome), but so he can live as God intended him to—in fullness and joy.

However, I know the dangers of poor theology. *Simply gloss over the wrongs that others have done to us, pretend they don't matter,* or worse*, ignore them as if they never happened.* This is a misguided belief that this is what forgiveness looks like, that this is what's meant by the verse which states, "love covers over a multitude of sins" (1 Pet. 4:8). It is not. Yes, love does cover a multitude of sins. But in the truest sense of the word, love and forgiveness must go hand in hand. You will not love someone well if you have not forgiven them. And it is impossible to forgive someone completely without first feeling, acknowledging, and expressing the pain they have caused you. It will not work otherwise. If you do not acknowledge your pain and allow yourself to feel it, it will not matter how many times you declare that you "forgive so-and-so in the name of Jesus." It will not happen.

You see, I have discovered that you cannot forgive someone until you know what you are forgiving them for. What you are forgiving them for is the pain, sometimes, deep, gut-wrenching pain that they have caused you to feel by their actions and decisions. If your mother tells you that she's unhappy with you for not yet giving her grandchildren, you cannot simply forgive her for hurting your feelings. You must forgive her for making you feel as though you have no value to her beyond the production of offspring, as though your life is not meaningful without children, as though she doesn't believe you capable of knowing when and under what circumstances having children would be the right decision for you and your spouse. I could go on. There are many layers. But you will not reach forgiveness if you do not see each of those layers, feel each one, and express your pain, anger, and devastation over each one of them—to God at the very least and hopefully to a trusted friend or partner.

This goes against the long-standing church tradition that says we are "good Christians" if we decide to "let go" of our anger in favor of "peace." Anger, however, is not wrong. It is a God-given tool. It is a signal, like a light on your car's dashboard, telling you something is amiss. Something needs addressing. We should not attempt to quickly rid ourselves of anger without proper process. We should look at it and dig and dig until we have discovered the painful reality about which we are truly angry. Once that thing has been identified, given permission to exist, and expressed, the anger will melt away all on its own—no white-knuckling will-power needed.

So, you see, when I communicate things about people in my life who have caused great pain to me, I am not in a place of anger or unforgiveness toward them. I have no desire to see my father's downfall or for him to "get what's coming to him." I hope what's coming to him is freedom, and I believe it is, if not in this world, then in the next. And yet, what God has taught me about suffering is so integrally related to my own experiences of it that I must discuss those experiences. I cannot be a "good Christian" and pretend they never happened. I must be a *real Christian* and give testimony to what God has actually healed within me. God does not require us to remain silent about our pain and abuse. He requires us not to slander, not to gossip, not to give false testimony. And as is the case with everything, God is concerned about the position of our hearts. In telling my story, I am not spreading information about those who have hurt me in an attempt to convince others to hate or be angry with them or to think less of them. In fact, I hope that by the end of this book, you will learn to view those people and the people who've hurt you through a radical lens of compassion and forgiveness as I have begun to do.

To return to the story of my father, I am very confident in my assessment of him as having all the qualifications to meet a diagnosis of narcissistic personality disorder. What this means is that my father has buried himself so deeply behind the façade he has built of who he believes he should be that he is incapable (under all normal circumstances) of even hearing that there might be room for him to grow, let alone actually taking the steps to do so. Please do not misunderstand. Narcissists are quite capable of appearing to admit wrongdoing, appearing to humbly say they have made a great many mistakes in their lives, but they are rarely, if ever, to be found admitting to the actual things they have done wrong or taking any sort of measurable action to correct those mistakes. I have heard my father (from the pulpit) admit to being an imperfect parent. I have never heard him in public or private admit to the actual actions he has taken against the well-being of his children, nor has he, up to the writing of this book, taken any notable or quantifiable steps to alter the long-standing unhealthy and abusive patterns of interaction in relationship to his children. He simply cannot do so without demolishing the entire structure upon which he has built his self-concept.

This meant that in my home growing up, every circumstance of his imperfect humanity must be blamed on someone else. My father could not be held responsible for one moment of defectiveness within the functioning of our family system. An example of this would be a time when one of my younger sisters was in my parents' kitchen, helping prepare a meal. My father pulled a large, scalding pan of food from the oven, and without looking, turned and rushed to set it on the counter. He ran straight into my sister, dumping the food on her arm. Her skin took the full brunt of the scalding juices from the pan. It was burned, red, swollen, and unable to be touched by any cloth for some time afterward. My father's response was to immediately and harshly reprimand her for being in his way, blaming her for what she had *done to him*. This type of scenario was a daily occurrence in my home growing up, a very normal one.

My father's inability to self-examine also meant that control was the most meaningful thing to him in life. He would sacrifice anything, any relationship, any dream, any monetary gain, to maintain control. As you can imagine, this was not a functional way to run a family, let alone a church. I have lost count of the number of church splits that took place in my father's church during my childhood and adolescence. All I knew was that one day I had friends, and the next day they were gone, and I was never permitted to see them again. In the family context, it meant that nearly every child in our family grew up hating our father. He was the villain of everyday life. His need for control often manifested itself through physical abuse. If you didn't do what he said the moment his sentence was completed, if you didn't look exceptionally thrilled about what he had instructed you to do, and for any other reason that struck his fancy, he would have no moral dilemma with shoving, hitting, slapping, pushing to the ground, kicking, and on occasion, punching his children, with the full belief this was appropriate and deserved. After all, we hadn't perfectly executed some task exactly as he had imagined it in his mind.

It wasn't only the physical abuse that defined my father's relationship with his children. The name-calling, degrading, diminishing comments about "how stupid a child has to be to make such-and-such a mistake" were constant. There was not a day when I didn't hear my father tell his children in no uncertain terms that they were useless, worthless, stupid, incompetent, a general waste of existence. I only heard positive comments directed toward me if I performed well in athletic competitions. On occasion, I heard him make a positive comment to someone else about my grades in school. That person invariably was unaware of the fact that I had no choice in the matter. Imperfection was dangerous.

I have known alcoholics or addicts who have abused their children under the influence of some substance and subsequently wept and apologized and felt acute shame about their actions after the fact. This was not my father. I believe I can confidently assert that he hasn't had a significant moment of disturbed conscience about his treatment of his children unless it seemed likely that someone outside the family might discover it, and it was all done in a perfectly sober state of mind.

Now, I don't want to make it sound as though my father did nothing positive whatsoever in my childhood. I can recognize how he attempted to be a better sort of man than his own father had been, which was, frankly, not a high bar. My father and all his siblings were horrifically abused by their father and neglected by their mother. My father tried to improve on this experience, and in some ways he did. Not necessarily, it appeared, in heart, but in actions. He built us a playhouse and read us books. He told us stories of his own invention. He had, at the very least, a touch of sentimentality about him that caused him to attempt to live up to his conceptualization of a "good father," even if there was a notable lack of real emotional engagement involved. There was a thin strand of humanity in him that I believe could have somehow been used to turn things around if he hadn't married my mother.

You see, the biggest thing in my life for which I needed to forgive my father was not his own abusive tendencies, but rather, for not protecting me from my mother. Though it was a difficult, painful, and time-consuming process for me to forgive my father, it was nothing compared with the depths of torment through which I had to tread in order to forgive my mother.

CHAPTER 3

Though my father and mother forsake me,
the Lord will receive me.

—Psalm 27:10

As it turned out, by my best ability to assess diagnostic criteria, my mother was *also* a narcissist. But she was a different breed of narcissist altogether. She was what has been termed in psychological research as a covert malignant narcissist. While my father was loud and obvious about his dysfunction at home and sometimes allowed the mask to slip a bit in public, my mother was very good at convincing the world that she was sweet and kind, gentle and sensitive, all the while, perpetrating the worst of abuses against her own offspring. Anyone who ever caught a glimpse of my father's shortcomings thought of my mother as a saint-like martyr for having been married to him for so many years. But I can assure you that, though I've met innumerable people throughout my life who have used manipulation as a primary means of interaction with others, I have never, in over forty years of life, met another human so manipulative as my mother. I have met people who are equally driven to manipulate, certainly, but never have I met someone who has so thoroughly succeeded in blinding the people within their sphere to their true state of existence. This was partially accomplished by my mother simply never allowing anyone close enough to her to see what was truly happening in her life and home. In my lifetime, my mother has never had an actual friend, and this was, quite clearly, by design.

My mother grew up in a Christian home. Her mother and father were first-generation believers. When I began to learn about narcissism, I understood that in order for my mother to have become a narcissist, she would have had to experience ongoing narcissistic abuse in her early life. My grandmother had highly narcissistic tendencies as well. However, she was largely ineffective in her attempts at abusive coercion because of the obviousness of her actions. She was not a sophisticated deceiver. Her motives were immediately apparent to anyone with an eye to recognize her preoccupation with control. Her grandchildren, myself included, would often roll their eyes and sigh loudly over her obnoxious attempts at boundary violations. But no one took her seriously. No one believed her to be a normal, healthy, functioning adult. Though I imagine this type of dysfunction would have caused significant interference in my mother's ability to develop normally all on its own, I knew that my mother didn't become the devious and deceptive person she was because of my grandmother. My mother's dysfunction appeared much greater and much deeper than my grandmother's and of a wholly different nature.

However, over the course of time, I learned a great deal about my mother's grandfather—the father of my grandmother. By all accounts from multiple relatives, he was utterly evil. Some of the information I present in this book will be difficult to read, but it is the true story of the suffering and sickness in my family line. My great-grandfather raped my grandmother regularly for most of her childhood and adolescence. He also sold her to other men for the same purpose. My grandmother, having blocked out the memories of her childhood from her mind, left her own children in the care of her parents while she worked. As you can imagine, he repeated the same patterns of perpetration on them that he had done to my grandmother.

My uncle died of a drug overdose when I was a young teen. It was clear that he was intimately acquainted with dark and difficult suffering. Addiction is a hallmark symptom of unhealed abuse, disconnection, and unsafe attachments in childhood. One of my aunts went through a difficult and painful healing process in adulthood, for which she was ridiculed and humiliated by my mother.

I was sexually abused by my mother regularly for the first few years of my life. I can only surmise the reasons that this ended, but I believe there were at least two notable events that took place in my mother's life that seemed to somewhat adjust her course when it came to the treatment of her children. The first situation that occurred was my father coming under investigation for the sexual abuse of a foster child living in our home—a girl nearly the same age as me. He was cleared in the end because, despite my father's faults, he would never sexually abuse a child. And I do not believe he was ever aware of my mother's abuse. I am convinced that the girl was being sexually abused in our home, but not by my father. I believe this incident frightened my mother with the realization that there could be real-life consequences for her actions toward her children. I have pondered the question of whether or not this incident actually caused my mother to truly consider for the first time the rightness or wrongness of this abuse. She was clearly an incredibly broken woman who spent every ounce of energy she had on either harmful domination of others or attempting to look perfect to the public. But such preoccupation with either of those goals is a very infantile mindset. I have come to believe that she had stopped emotionally maturing at a very young age because of the abuse she suffered. The higher-functioning mind of an adult who considers right and wrong had never been a part of her paradigm to that point. I find it entirely feasible that this was the first time she even contemplated whether abusing her children would be considered wrong, having spent her life in a state of emotionally driven pursuit of domination and control to combat the feelings of powerlessness she experienced from her own childhood abuse.

Another notable occurrence in my mother's life that seemed to slightly shift her course was, I believe, having read the book *A Child Called "It"* by Dave Pelzer. It was a popular book for a time, and the author went into great detail about the horrific abuse he experienced at the hands of his mother. I believe that my mother once again came face to face with the reality that things done in the dark often become exposed in the light, and it frightened her. Prior to this, I doubt she had contemplated what her own children might have to say about her once they were out from under her thumb. Again, I think she realized for the first time that her tactics of abusive control and domination (quite similar to the mother described in this book in a number of ways) were considered morally reprehensible by society at large, which caused her to contemplate her use of such tactics for the first time in her life. Thankfully, none of my younger siblings were born yet when my mother appears to have had her initial encounters with the reality of her actions, so it is my belief that they did not experience the same level of destruction of soul that accompanied the sexual abuse I experienced at our mother's hands. They were abused, make no mistake, some horrifically so. But their lives do not appear to have borne the fruit of the level of violation caused by sexual abuse from a parent, and none of them has ever, to my knowledge, claimed to experience such things at her hands.

There was at least one other person, a man, by whom I was sexually abused. There may have been others. I'm not certain. I came to full remembrance of this abuse from my mother during my own process of healing, just as my grandmother had near the end of her life, when she had a renewed awareness of the painful memories of childhood abuse by her father. All of my life I knew I had been sexually abused, and it bore out in my life in many clear ways, not least of which was the constant, heavy, oppressive sense of being filthy, tainted, disgusting, and shameful. I have no memories of life until quite recently without that demonic spirit and associated self-hatred present. I had knowledge of sexual concepts for the entire expanse of my memory, only in later years of adolescence having the intellectual capacity to understand the implications of this awareness.

On top of the sexual abuse, however, and well after it was over (up to the writing of this book), my mother was responsible for perpetrating the worst and most damaging types of emotional and psychological abuse on her children, most especially my older sister and me, and many years later, several of my much younger siblings. She lived to break us. Even in the moments she pretended to be kind, it was only ever for the purpose of slipping in a degrading comment or manipulating us into giving her something she wanted, or, on occasion, to impress some nearby observer into believing she was a doting mother. Every word she spoke, every action she took was for the sole purpose of making us believe that we were worthless, undeserving of her attention, beneath her.

She spent the bulk of her energy outside of tormenting her children devising ways to make herself appear wonderful to the "public." This usually meant the people at our church. She wanted to appear to be the perfect mother, so she homeschooled us, which was considered a very holy thing to do at that time. The primary difficulty with this scenario (other than my siblings and I being trapped at home with our abuser) was that she didn't actually teach us anything. The one positive thing I remember about my childhood was that I could disappear into the woods for an entire day at a time, and no one would notice my absence (or care even if they did). This allowed me some safety, but very little academic preparation for later in life when I attended an actual school. All of my academic skills were well below age level when I began attending school because of my mother's refusal to educate us at home. You see, homeschooling us was only to look good; she didn't want to actually *do* anything for us. Thankfully, I was an intelligent child, and that combined with my terror of imperfection allowed me to catch up quickly. Eventually, I graduated from high school as the valedictorian of my class.

My parents bought into the popular theological perspective of the time that dictated that a wife was always to submit to her husband (they liked to gloss over the verses about submitting to each other). This worked well for my mother because manipulation was the only communication tool she had acquired in life, and the damaging evangelical system of wife-only submission promotes and also creates controlling husbands and manipulative wives. God designed people to be powerful, to have choice, voice, and freedom. When they aren't permitted freedom, they still have a need to be powerful, so they try to meet that need through manipulation and control directed toward others instead of healthy self-regulation. People who grow up in a system like this are only comfortable when they attain power through manipulation instead of open, honest communication. So, the toxic wife-submission ideology provides the perfect solution for both manipulative women and domineering men. Often the manipulative women will be the hardest to convince of another model for marriage because they are terrified of having to communicate with others in a way that is powerful and genuine. My mother was one of these. As a result, I grew up believing that women were second-class citizens. Humans were made in the image of God, but only men were created in the *real* image of God. Women were included in the statement because God was trying to be nice. This was the general idea of things.

I have more fingers than I have memories of my mother showing me physical affection in childhood. Of those memories, all were minimal and generally took place in public settings where she thought it made her appear to be a good mother. However, I have innumerable memories of my mother slapping me, ripping out my hair, whipping me with leather belts, digging her nails deeply into my skin, and squeezing my arm so hard that marks were left. I came to understand that her touch was to be feared, not sought, avoided at all costs. As a person who ranks physical touch quite high on my love language scale, you can imagine the confusion I've had to overcome to even begin to understand healthy physical affection. I primarily have my own children to thank for launching me into this journey of healing and understanding when it comes to physical affection. Being physically affectionate with them came so naturally to me that I, on some level, taught myself what a mother might look like who actually carried love in her heart for her children.

However, the physical pain my mother caused was nothing compared to the psychological torment. Often, she would create scenarios where the only possible outcome was my failure. Then, she could enjoy watching me desperately try to meet her expectations only to convince me that she was justified in verbally humiliating me for my inevitable failure. On many occasions, there wasn't even a task she had set me to do. She simply felt the desire to emotionally torment me. She would walk in on me performing some innocent task, such as playing with a toy or combing my hair, and begin to rail against me for how wrongly I was doing whatever it was, how I must be stupid, useless, worthless in order to do such-and-such in this way. I learned to listen for footsteps and tones of voice in other rooms. I learned to be vigilant constantly, reading the minutest changes in facial expressions, body posture, or movements in an attempt to predict when and how the next barrage of shame or pain might come.

Another difficult factor at play in my childhood, one that I would not have fully confirmed until much later in adulthood, was the fact that I was autistic. This type of neurodivergence is, thankfully, much more readily tested for and diagnosed in today's world than during my childhood. When I was a child, it was thought to be exceedingly rare and believed that only boys could be autistic. Even if times had been different, there is little chance I would have received a diagnosis or any assistance in navigating a hopelessly overstimulating world in childhood. Why? My only reason for existing, according to my mother's worldview, was to make her look good, and having any attribute that was not highly regarded by society would not have made her look good. As nothing more than an extension of her, I was to be perfect, so as to display her own state of perfection. As it was, I made a great number of social mistakes in my early years and was punished and shamed unrelentingly for them until I learned that silence was safer than to risk saying something wrong or in the wrong way or with the wrong tone of voice.

I was shamed for any expression of emotion by my mother and sometimes my father, but especially if that expression was to communicate that I felt pain of any kind, physical or emotional. I heard daily from my mother to "stop being so sensitive," the real implication being that I needed to *stop being myself*. My earliest memory is from a time when I was not yet a steady walker, so quite young. I was walking through the living room of my home when I smashed my foot hard against the leg of our coffee table. My parents were both sitting on the couch. I was in terrible pain. I sat down, holding my foot, looking at my injured toe, crying. I looked to my parents for some sort of acknowledgment of my pain. My mother began to point at me and laugh. It wasn't a genuine laugh. It was a laugh intended to communicate ridicule. I don't remember the words she said exactly, but I know what they meant. "You are crying because of pain. You are pathetic and should be ashamed." She then turned to my father and convinced him to join in on mocking me with a pretense of laughter for my tears. I felt such confusion, such devastation. I was in pain. Weren't these people supposed to care about that? They did not. And, I am quite convinced, there was never a subsequent pain in my life about which either of my parents had the slightest concern. I do not say this for the sake of dramatic effect. I assure you it is an accurate statement of my reality. I do not have a single memory of crying about physical pain after this experience until the age of forty.

So, when lights were too bright, noises too loud, and people too many, I learned to silently sit in them and suffer. When we were at another family's house and I was offered food or a drink, I learned to graciously decline no matter how thirsty or hungry I was, because the consequences of "asking for things" from other people (even when I did not ask, but only accepted) were disastrous. I was to have no needs, no feelings, no humanity. I was not to exist other than as a prop to my mother's play. She was the heroine. I was her chair, her dress, her mirror, nothing more. "I'm okay," and "I'm fine," were the two most common phrases spoken from my mouth. But I was neither.

CHAPTER 4

...but there is a friend who sticks closer than a brother.
—Proverbs 18:24

It would be reasonable to think that my older sister and I might have bonded in childhood over our shared experiences of abuse and suffering, empathized with one another, provided some connection to replace the one missing with our parents. Sadly, we did not. I have no memories of a time in my formative years of not knowing that my sister despised me. She had been tormented by our mother and had a volatile relationship with her for all of my life—well into adulthood.

There are four primary ways that humans instinctively respond to threats: the commonly known fight or flight and the lesser-known freeze and fawn. There were very few things in my life that my nervous system did not perceive as a threat. It was usually correct in its assessment. My automatic response to threats was first to freeze and then to silently, carefully slip away unnoticed to avoid danger (flight). My sister's primary response to threat was fight. This created a situation in which she and my mother were constantly in a battle over who was in control. No matter how hard she was hit, no matter what awful, evil things my mother said about her or did to her, she would not back down, even in very early childhood. This resulted in a great deal of violence between the two. Besides physical violence, I have never heard the likes of the evil things said by my mother to my sister, and, later on, by my sister to my mother, in any other arguments I have ever witnessed in my life, and I have seen a great many hostile disagreements.

It was an unfortunate truth that my sister did not only see my mother as a threat but also appeared to perceive me in the same way. I was over two years younger than her and much smaller, but she decided the day I was born that I was a danger to her existence and treated me accordingly. There was a fair amount of physical harm, yes, but the skills that she learned from my mother for how to inflict the greatest amount of emotional damage in the fewest words were practiced on me daily. She made it her life goal to make certain that I knew I was absolutely beneath her, unimportant, worthless. For example, at an early age, I began to draw and paint as the only means available to me to express my emotions in safety. I would spend hours drawing pictures meticulously, ensuring that every detail was exactly how it was meant to look. My sister would often find creative ways to destroy my artwork and make it appear to be my fault. If I was drawing on the floor, she would go out of her way to step on my papers and grind them into the floor, telling me I shouldn't have been drawing where she wanted to walk. If I was drawing on the table, she would find ways to spill things on my papers, knock them on the floor, rip them "accidentally" and tell me I should have had them somewhere else because she wanted to set her cup there.

Whenever there was only one of something available, it belonged to her without discussion. There was not even a question. She daily told me all the ways she was better than me, smarter, stronger, prettier. This lasted even into early adulthood. If a man showed romantic interest in me, she would be sure to let me know that she "could have had him," but she didn't want him, and this was the only reason he was interested in me. I could fill a chapter of this book with the degrading names she called me in childhood alone.

I never had such feelings toward her, however, and never treated her with contempt, so she began to confide in me about her emotional difficulties. I would sit and listen to her speak for hours about her feelings (she is a verbal processor), but I learned quickly that I could not expect the same consideration from her. On the few occasions when I attempted to confide in her in childhood or adolescence, I regretted it immensely, as she would always find a way to use that information against me later to degrade and embarrass me. In later years of adulthood, our relationship improved significantly. Unfortunately, my early childhood brain development was well over by this point in time, and many difficult-to-break patterns firmly set.

CHAPTER 5

*And we know that in all things God works for the
good of those who love him, who have been called
according to his purpose.*

—Romans 8:28

You may begin to imagine that I have some understanding of suffering.

I became what is called in the world of psychology a *co-dependent*. I allowed myself to be mistreated, taken advantage of, ignored, and in all ways used throughout my lifetime. The notion that I was not a human and did not have any rights had been so ingrained in me that I did not recognize abuse as abuse when it occurred. Additionally, as my parents and my older sister were my primary attachment figures in early childhood, my brain had unwittingly wired itself to believe that connection was only to be found in people who mistreated, damaged, and abused me. Having had no choice in the fact that I must get my survival needs met by the very same people who daily caused me excruciating pain resulted in my brain and my soul believing the only place where needs could be met was in volatile, destructive, and hate-fueled relationships. As a result, I attracted one abusive man after another. A series of broken relationships left me in even more pieces than my family of origin had.

We will never allow ourselves to be loved to a greater degree than we love ourselves, and so I consistently found excuses to avoid relationships with healthy men or healthy people in general. They were "boring," "judgmental," and "shallow." We had nothing in common. The fact of the matter was that I was not drawn to healthy people because I was afraid of them. I knew how to survive in dysfunction, abuse, and pain. The world of stability and love was so foreign to me that all the work I had done to learn how to stay alive in an abusive environment would have been worthless and wasted in an environment of health. All the skills I had painstakingly developed would have taken me nowhere, and, in my mind, it would not have taken a healthy person long to see me for what I was: completely unlovable, worthless, and subhuman. At least my connections with highly broken individuals were likely to last longer, as I could convince them that I *was* worth their effort and interest for a greater length of time. It was harder for them to see through my mask to the ugliness within because they were blinded by their own.

This approach, however, did not ultimately produce my intended results. Even having escaped my parents' home in adulthood, my life remained a series of one crushing blow after another.

I remember a time believing that I was going to die as I lay on the floor of my house, blackness beginning to fill in my field of vision as my college boyfriend, who weighed nearly 250 pounds, sat on top of me and choked me into the floor. For reference, I am 5'2" and at my heaviest have never weighed more than 135 pounds. At that moment, something clicked in my brain, and I knew I wanted better, even if I didn't really deserve it (as I believed). I determined that if I came out of that situation alive, I would not get into another one like it again. Unfortunately, the next long-term relationship I entered was with the man who would ultimately become my husband and the father of my children. On the outside, he seemed entirely different than the man before him, whom I had had to leave the country to escape. He was not. They were cut from the same cloth, and it was ultimately the disintegration of that marriage that launched me into my journey of healing and facing down all of the ugly pain.

That college boyfriend was responsible for my first experience of sexual intercourse as an adult. It was not consensual, and for that, I blamed myself as I had learned to do so early on.

At the age of twenty, I developed my first chronic health condition. I did not realize it at the time, but my nervous system had been in "fight-or-flight" (and in my case, freeze) mode from birth, possibly before, which meant the system that was supposed to occasionally activate during dire, life-threatening circumstances was turned on every second of every day. When this happens, the effects on the body are disastrous. It began with Chronic Fatigue Syndrome, which developed from having caught the mononucleosis virus in college. It was followed by a series of health conditions that developed and simply never left. Gout, cystitis, an unnamed autoimmune disease, tendonitis in my hands, polycystic ovarian syndrome, endometriosis, skin cancer, extreme hormonal disorders, and sleep disorders to name some.

During my two pregnancies, I had hyperemesis, a condition that caused me to feel extreme nausea without a moment of relief and to vomit, sometimes dozens of times per day, for the entire nine months of each pregnancy, resulting in hospitalizations and panic attacks. Because of my other experiences with health conditions, I spent my pregnancies terrified that the condition would not leave once I had given birth to my children (it did thankfully).

Besides the physical conditions I developed as a result of my fight-or-flight system being perpetually turned on, I also experienced significant emotional and relational difficulties in younger years both because of my daily encounters with emotional abuse and because of my autism. I had a long history of being alone. I never had any real friends in childhood besides my own siblings because, in order to be real friends with someone, you have to be able to share personal information about your life. The consequences I would have faced had I told a soul about any of my parents' abusive behaviors were not worth the potential benefits of friendship, and so I spent my life alone and friendless by any meaningful definition of the word "friend." Because of my autism and because of the nature of my relationships with my mother and older sister, I was utterly incapable of forming friendships with other girls and women, a source of great pain to me throughout my life.

My nervous system was even wired to respond to my own mistakes as a threat. To this day, I am still in the process of retraining my physical brain and nervous system not to be triggered into gut-wrenching fear when I make a social mistake. Because of the way the autistic brain

31

works, I was much more naturally geared toward connecting with other humans in ways that were more typical of boys and men than of women. I excelled in athletic competitions and hyper-focus on projects. I seemed to always be accidentally insulting people. The most notable difference in my peer groups was that the girls seemed inclined to be eternally offended by my unintended insults, whereas the boys seemed to rather enjoy the process of being insulted. I was not easily offended by teasing or pranks, and so learned quickly how to form some level of connection with boys my age. Additionally, since my father only ever praised me for things that he saw as masculine traits (whereas my mother seemingly praised me for nothing), I focused most on developing those skills.

This did not go over well with the girls my age, however. I was constantly rejected by other girls in my peer groups. Often, I would have liked to be friends with them but was unable to understand or successfully imitate their methods of relationship-building. They always seemed affronted by my straightforward way of communicating, offended that I had other interests besides things they were interested in, offended that I so easily got along with the boys my age, offended that those boys seemed to enjoy my company. I was accused of being rude if I tried to genuinely communicate, accused of being "stuck-up" and arrogant if I kept silent. There was many a birthday party in high school when every girl in my small school was invited with the exception of me, many rude comments meant to "put me in my place" for thinking I was better than others (this was the furthest thing from being the real issue), many a hushed conversation that ended with girls in my class laughing and pointing in my direction, intending for me to see them. The message was once again clear: who I am is unacceptable, wrong, undesirable.

In order to be accepted, I would have to alter the very fabric of who I was. I did try. For years I tried. I memorized conversations to make sure I sounded "normal" when having interactions, I practiced giving compliments, laughing at jokes, talking enthusiastically about things I found uninteresting, and forcing myself to be uncomfortable so that I didn't look weird trying to adjust my clothing or move my body to a comfortable position.

Because of these types of experiences and those of my mother's explosive reactions to my social mistakes, I began to constantly run a background program in my brain during every interaction with another human being besides (eventually) my children. This program was constantly monitoring every movement, action, and breath I took to determine if they were things that would be considered mistakes of social expectations or not. "Am I sitting weird? Does my voice sound normal? Am I expressing enough distress in this response? Will it be weird for me to get up and use the bathroom right now? Did I interject at an acceptable moment in the conversation? Is anyone else here moving their hands as much as I am?" I am still in the process of untraining my brain from the use of this program. My already-existent hypervigilance was exacerbated greatly by the need to always figure out what actions and words would be socially acceptable in a given situation.

Despite the fact that I have always loved learning new skills and information, the fear of social ostracization prevented me from having the courage to try new things, especially if doing so involved unknown social rules. Instead, I focused my energy on developing new skills and knowledge I could acquire and enjoy alone. I believed myself to be an extreme introvert. However, was the relief I felt when alone at least in part due to my crushing fear of social mistakes? Was the inevitable exhaustion of spending time in the presence of others because my brain was constantly monitoring every miniscule movement of my body and face?

It took until my late thirties to realize that it was all wasted effort. Not one of those girls or women ended up liking or accepting me after all of the years I put into trying to seem normal. Not one. I have had no lifelong friendships with other women besides my own siblings. In fact, I have spent the majority of my life in a state sometimes known as pathological loneliness—a deep aching pit of emptiness where love and connection should have been. I was not consciously aware that I lived in pathological loneliness. Believing I was "fine," my actions told a different story if I had only known how to interpret them. In adulthood, I have gone for long periods, once nearly a year, without touching another human being and did not consciously feel the loss, despite later learning that touch was one of my topmost love languages. For years at a time I've gone without crying because of the extent to which I was trained to dissociate from my own needs and feelings. I once played soccer for nearly six months with a broken foot—a sad example of my deep conditioning to ignore the signals of my own body's needs and pain.

I was chronically unable to share a bed or even a bedroom with another human being for most of my life because my nervous system perceived the presence of any other person as a threat and could not calm enough to fall asleep. This included my husband (who *was* very much a threat) and even my children.

On top of all of this, I grew up in a church that was deeply entrenched in the shame- and fear-based approach to sexuality known as purity culture. I cannot count the number of times I heard women who were not virgins referred to as "damaged goods," "used cars," "chewed gum," and other similar analogies. Ironically, my mother, who had sexually assaulted me regularly in early childhood, was the biggest proponent of this philosophy. If there was shame involved, she wanted on that wagon.

As you can imagine, I was largely a wide-open target for demonic oppression. Growing up, I had heard of how terrible of a person Mary Magdelene must have been before meeting Christ. After all, she had seven demons that Jesus had to drive out of her. I laugh now when I think of it. What I would have given to *only* have seven demons.

I have carried the weight of disease and disability in my own children, rejection and hatred within the body of Christ, debilitating fear of man, the shame of wrongs I have done to others in my own state of brokenness, loss of people, loss of dreams, betrayal, lies told about me and those I told myself, divorce, single parenthood (including the shame of not being enough to fill two roles), loss of physical abilities, addiction, damaging soul-ties, financial lack, isolation, demonic oppression, and a host of other difficulties I could list. On the official psychological side of things, I have had PTSD, CPTSD, co-dependency, a fearful-avoidant (disorganized) attachment system, depression, anxiety, sexual dysfunction, and more.

There is far more that I could add to the account of my own personal experiences with suffering, but my primary purpose in writing this book is not to give an in-depth account of my life story. My hope is that using my own experiences of suffering and the process of healing from it can help others navigate their own journeys toward wholeness in Christ. I hope that in this broad overview of the various types of suffering I have experienced in life, people reading this book will find something to which they can relate and hopefully understand that their pain, their suffering, is also able to be healed.

Your ashes can be exchanged for beauty, as so much of mine have been.

Maturity

CHAPTER 6

Let perseverance finish its work so that you may be mature and complete, not lacking anything.

—James 1:4

The church has done a poor job when it comes to the topic of suffering, from claiming that God is the author of our suffering, to the equally incomplete claim that He has no part in it. Neither of these extremes is adequate to provide a full understanding of the topic.

It is simply untrue, and frankly, unbiblical, to claim that God initiates, inspires, or allows sickness, abuse, and a host of other harmful experiences of suffering in the lives of individuals. It is equally as untrue to state that God does not require us to suffer in this life. Look at Jesus. The central focus of His mission on this earth was to suffer and die. Certainly, He did a great many other important things while here, but the ultimate goal of His life was accomplished through suffering, and, in fact, His own murder. He was sent here for that purpose. How many times did He warn His disciples that He must suffer and be killed before it took place? How many prophecies from the Old Testament spoke about the suffering Jesus would endure in this life? This was not coincidence, happenstance, or a byproduct of His being born as a man. It was the very point. It was the path required of Him in order to accomplish the task for which He was sent to earth. Carrying the weight of every sin ever committed was never going to be light work. There was no pain-free method to achieve the salvation of humanity.

Isaiah 53:1 says of Jesus, "He was despised and rejected by men, a man of sorrows, and familiar with suffering. Like one from whom men hide their faces he was despised, and we esteemed him not. Surely he took up our infirmities and carried our sorrows, yet we considered him stricken by God, smitten by him, and afflicted."

This verse quite succinctly shows two things: the fact that Jesus' suffering was integral to His mission on this earth, and also that God Himself does not desire our pain or sickness. Christ experienced unthinkable suffering, and through it, God offered healing to us. So, the precedent for God requiring suffering during earthly life is set, as well as the fact that the healing and restoration of our own suffering is the longing of his heart. If we are to be like Jesus, then why should we be exempt from experiencing suffering? Why should we assume God does not call us to experience a certain level of suffering as an essential piece of accomplishing our individual missions in life too? Even so, this does not contradict the fact that His purpose is to make healing available to us. His goal for us is not to remain in a state of suffering, even if some level of suffering is required of us; His goal is our wholeness.

Now, I do not claim that any human will have nearly as great a call and purpose on his or her life as Jesus Christ. No human could possibly have borne the weight of all the sin of all of humankind throughout history as Jesus did. If they could, we would not have so desperately needed Him.

But I will say that I agree with the assertion of Bill Johnson and other leaders in the modern Charismatic church who teach that Jesus is perfect theology. We are called to be like Him, to do the things He has done and greater things, according to the Bible. Of course this involves enforcing the Kingdom of Heaven through healing, resurrection, miracles, signs, and wonders. Of course it involves freedom, victory, and deliverance. I believe it also involves a requirement of suffering. Now, I mean this in a general sense, not that God designs specific instances of suffering in our lives (except under narrow conditions to be discussed later in this book). But I do believe He asks us to partake in this life of suffering *unto something*. Jesus' suffering was unto salvation for humanity, primarily. Our suffering is unto something as well. Our suffering has the potential to impact our mission on this earth as it relates to other people, certainly. But, in a general sense, it's also unto the accomplishing of a significant work within us—namely, maturity.

How many places in the Bible is our need for and the benefits of maturity highlighted? How many places is our need to become immune to the influences of the world, false doctrines, and our own temptations discussed?

Ephesians 4:11–16 states:

So Christ himself gave the apostles, the prophets, the evangelists, the pastors and teachers, to equip his people for works of service, so that the body of Christ may be built up until we all reach unity in the faith and in the knowledge of the Son of God and become mature, attaining to the whole measure of the fullness of Christ.

Then we will no longer be infants, tossed back and forth by the waves, and blown here and there by every wind of teaching and by the cunning and craftiness of people in their deceitful scheming. Instead, speaking the truth in love, we will grow to become in every respect the mature body of him who is the head, that is, Christ. From him the whole body, joined and held together by every supporting ligament, grows and builds itself up in love, as each part does its work.

Hebrews 5:13–14 tells us:

Anyone who lives on milk, being still an infant, is not acquainted with the teaching about righteousness. But solid food is for the mature, who by constant use have trained themselves to distinguish good from evil.

First Corinthians 2:6 says:

We do, however, speak a message of wisdom among the mature, but not the wisdom of this age or of the rulers of this age, who are coming to nothing.

And if we read the book of James chapter 1, we simply cannot deny that God very clearly connects difficulty and suffering with the process of maturity:

Consider it pure joy, my brothers and sisters whenever you face trials of many kinds, because you know that the testing of your faith produces perseverance. Let perseverance finish its work so that you may be mature and complete, not lacking anything.

Not only does He connect maturity to suffering, but we are instructed to consider it *a joy* when we experience suffering *because* of the results it produces in us: maturity and completion. Again, we must not fall into the harmful belief that God initiates specific instances of suffering in our lives to teach us lessons. We must, however, strike a balance, a tension, between the understanding that God does not cause our suffering, and He intensely desires our freedom and healing, and at the same time does require a level of suffering to be a part of our human experience in this life for the purpose of our own maturity. You see, God does not fit nicely into either extreme theological camp. He fits precisely where the truth lies—a place of both love and kindness and also challenge and difficulty.

But why is God so focused on maturity in us? To start with, He hopes to spend eternity in a mature relationship with us.

As a parent with a child who has already reached adulthood, as well as children who I am still raising, I am acutely aware of how my relationship with my adult daughter, who is nearly a decade older than her next sibling, is vastly different than my relationship with my younger children. And our relationship is vastly different now than our relationship was when she was much younger. Though I find myself reminiscing about the days when my children were babies or when they did adorable things in younger childhood, I would not return to those years if given the choice. The more mature my children become, the more of my heart, my thoughts, and my dreams I can share with them, the more I can trust them with certain knowledge and information, and the more I can trust them to be responsible with things that are important to me and beneficial for them. Also, and of the greatest importance, the more I begin to see them discover who they are and begin to walk out the things God has placed within them. In adulthood, my oldest daughter has often blessed me as much as I feel I have blessed her. I can share with her spiritual revelations and personal journeys that my younger children are not yet capable of bearing. This is God's desire for us as well. He longs to share with us more of His heart and His dreams and for us to be able to carry the weight of more of His glory into the earth, to spend eternity with us in a mature state.

A second reason that God desires our maturity is because we are meant to reign over the earth with Him for all of time. We are to have dominion over the earth as God initially gave to Adam and Eve. No parent would entrust the running of their estate to a young child. It would not even be legally permitted to do so because even the human systems of law recognize the need for maturity to reliably carry out significant responsibility. The parable of the talents (Matthew 25:14–30) shows us that what we do with what we are given determines our level of authority at a later designated time. I strongly suspect that this parable is referencing mainly what we do with this lifetime. The reward those servants were given was to rule over certain numbers of cities. It appears likely to me that our level of authority on the new earth in eternity is directly tied to how we've managed this life and how much maturity and authority we have developed in it.

I do not believe the presence of the serpent in the Garden of Eden was necessary for Adam and Eve to have eventually eaten from the Tree of the Knowledge of Good and Evil. After all, Satan did not have an evil entity tempting him when he chose to abandon his Creator in favor of his own pride. Free will appears to be enough on its own to eventuate disobedience. But I believe a large part of why the devil and his minions are permitted to remain on the earth during the current age is to give us the opportunity to mature into our authority, to learn to begin to take dominion over the earth and over darkness. We will need this level of maturity and authority if we are to rule the new earth wisely and responsibly. And I believe the thing that left Adam and Eve with the greatest susceptibility to the words of the serpent was their immaturity. They were perfectly created beings, brilliant and full of life. But they were not mature.

The Bible tells us immaturity causes us to be swayed by every wind of doctrine we encounter (Eph. 4:11–16), to be convinced of one strange belief after another and not hold fast to the truth. And that is what happened to Adam and Eve. They were quickly and easily swayed by persuasive words because they lacked maturity. They walked with God daily, interacted with Him at a level that we ourselves are not likely to see until eternity. And yet, this was not enough to make them mature. No amount of time living in perfection would have created maturity in them, even when their time was spent in the very presence of the Creator. They never had any obstacles to overcome. There was never any faith required of them because they already saw. They were never required to stand firm in the knowledge of God's goodness in the face of circumstances that suggested otherwise. And so, they were quickly and easily convinced by the first being who showed up to offer an alternative explanation of existence. And I do believe that, though God did not desire Adam and Eve to be disobedient or to experience suffering, He did desire them to become mature.

Honestly, the parallels to the crucifixion of Jesus are striking. When Jesus was killed, the devil believed he had won a great victory. He believed God's plan to save humanity was thwarted, when, in fact, he had driven human beings to accomplish the very thing that God had set out for Jesus to do. God would not have slain His own Son, tortured, or maimed Him. It is not in His nature. He cannot act outside of His nature. And so, I believe God also allows the forces of darkness to remain in the earth for this time to use them for His purposes.

There is precedent for this idea in Scripture. How many evil kings did God say that He chose to use as His vessels to accomplish the discipline of Israel in the Old Testament? The king of Babylon and the king of Assyria, to name two prominent ones. And we know God used Judas to accomplish His purpose in Jesus' death. Though God has granted free will even to evil people, this does not mean that He is unable to use even the actions of such free-willed individuals to accomplish His purposes.

It appears to me that God's purpose and desire was always for our maturity. However, we can know simply from raising children that maturity does not come without obstacles to overcome and difficulties to face. I would like to suggest that when the serpent deceived Adam and Eve, he was accomplishing a necessary step in the process of the maturation and growth of humanity. Woe to him through whom it came though, just like Judas. God was not pleased with Adam and Eve's disobedience. He was not pleased with the serpent's deception of them. There were consequences to all three of their choices, as there always is for choosing sin. But it was necessary to accomplish the work in humanity that God set out to complete.

This is a hard idea to accept or even contemplate. Hard, but good, which are the words I have come to use most often to describe the ways of God. The more layers I peel back in understanding the story of God's design for our existence, the more deeply loved and cherished I feel by Him, even in the face of harsh and painful reality.

CHAPTER 7

Anyone who lives on milk, being still an infant,
is not acquainted with the teaching about righteousness.

—Hebrews 5:13

One of the most common reasons that atheists give for having greater faith in the ludicrous notion of life spontaneously erupting into existence than in the idea that life and physical matter were designed by a being superior to ourselves is the presence of suffering. A good God would not allow His creation to suffer, they say. In particular, they point to the suffering of those they deem innocent: children, animals, and people who are kind and generous and clearly not "deserving" of suffering. How could a God who is good allow such people to experience the anguish of suffering that can be felt in this life?

In his book, *The Problem of Pain*, C.S. Lewis's poignant response to this question is to ask instead where on earth we humans would have gotten the idea that suffering should not exist if God doesn't exist. What on earth would have given us the idea that there is some *other way* that human beings should experience life than the way in which we do? No other animals on earth question why their kind are eaten by larger, more powerful predators. Where on earth did this moral notion that suffering is wrong and should not exist come from if, in fact, there is no objective standard of right and wrong? In other words, what would have made us believe there should not be suffering in the world, that the way things are is not the way they are supposed to be? If Darwin's "survival of the fittest" is to be believed, then we should accept the death of the old, weak, sickly, and disabled as a natural, even beneficial occurrence to the greater good of society, right? But we do not. No, we have a deeply ingrained sense that there is some other way of existing that's superior to what we currently experience. Where did such an idea come from?

The very basis of many atheists' arguments is, in and of itself, an argument for a Creator.

However, atheism itself is not often based in critical thinking. So, the conclusion is that either God is not good, or He does not exist. Such a statement certainly appeals to our emotions. What parent doesn't try to prevent their child from experiencing any and all suffering? Well, for one, a parent who desires their child to someday be a functional adult who is capable of mature decision-making.

It is true that helicopter parenting, which seeks to prevent children from having normal experiences of difficulty or pain in their lives at all costs, has become a popular method of raising children in recent times. Parents have become so obsessed with "safety" over all other aspects of life that children no longer experience the exploration, independence, and freedom necessary for healthy emotional, mental, and physical development. It's not a coincidence now that parents have stopped allowing their children to climb too high, run too fast, play with toy weapons, and wrestle each other in the dirt there has been a dramatic rise in depression and anxiety in younger and younger populations, a measurable drop in resiliency in those just beginning to enter adulthood, and formidable reduction in balance and motor skills in older children as compared to previous generations. There are certainly other contributing factors at play, but a significant contributing factor is that children have stopped participating in normal, healthy levels of risk-taking in childhood, which often result in skinned knees, bruises, and sometimes even broken bones. However, this also results in better physical balance, stamina, coordination, and overall health, as well as the ability to accurately assess risk, make well-thought-out decisions, critically assess information, and the confidence necessary to try new things absent the debilitating fear of failure or danger.

The desperate need for the children of today to learn and understand the natural consequences of their decisions cannot be overstated. The lack of this understanding has resulted in a generation of young people who are afraid of everything. They do not want to be bosses; they want someone to tell them what to do. They do not trust their own abilities or decisions. They are terrified of what would, a short time ago, have been considered normal requirements of adulthood and life in general. And what will happen when those who are bosses now retire, when the terrified generation is all that's left to run the world's enterprises? They will be easily controllable to any voice that will give them direction. Easily swayed by any doctrine, philosophy, or theory that seems to give them some direction to follow. It has already begun.

As a parent, I have often cringed at the potential for painful injuries that could occur from my children's activities. But knowing what I know about critical stages of development in children, I determined early on to staunchly hold my tongue when they climbed to the tops of trees, hung upside down on monkey bars, dug in the dirt and mud, and many other forms of what used to be considered normal childhood risk-taking. The number of times I have had neighbors knock on my door and ask, "Did you know your children are doing such and such?" is beyond counting. The number of other adults who have attempted to tell my children to stop activities that they deemed "unsafe" while I was a matter of feet away is absurd.

In the world we live in, it's difficult for many people to conceive of a loving parent allowing their children to do anything with even a slight potential for injury, but for millennia of human history, this was not the case. The people of ancient times, right up until a few short decades ago, had no cognitive dissonance over a God who allowed His children to blunder into difficult or painful situations and was always there to guide them out of those situations should they choose to ask for His help.

Until recent years, the idea that it is God's responsibility to keep us "safe" from any form of difficulty or pain would have been considered laughable at best. During normal stages of early human development, babies often cling to their mothers, afraid of the world around them. But as their bodies become steadier and they begin to feel more confident and know what to expect from the world, they begin to experiment. They begin to explore. And the natural progression is that eventually, they begin to refuse their mother's assistance in their explorations. They want to do it themselves. They fall often. They get many bumps, bruises, and scrapes. They return to their mother for comfort, but just as quickly attempt the same activity until they have mastered it. This is resiliency.

If a mother were to prevent her child from attempting to walk because of the potential for injury, she would rightly be considered abusive. Eventually, she would have to restrain the child to keep it from attempting the skill. We would instinctively know that this mother was preventing a necessary, foundational step in the child's process of development for no other purpose than to avoid her own emotional discomfort at seeing her child experience minor, recoverable pain. We instinctively know the responsibility of a loving parent is not to absolutely prevent their children from experiencing any pain, but it is to help guide their children through situations where they do experience it.

A child begins to experiment and crave independence very early, well below one year of age in most children. But many modern cultures have reverted to an infantile developmental stage where we desire safety above healthy development. The emotional plea of the average atheist saying that God is not good or isn't real because we sometimes experience difficulty is sadly just that—an infantile mentality. I say this without judgment. It is truly heartbreaking. Those who hold such an underdeveloped view of existence are in desperate need of exactly the kind of love that is offered by our Creator and that should also be offered by us: transformational love. Unconditional love cannot help but spur us on to greater, better, and often even more difficult (but wonderful) things in life. This is growth.

Sadly, many Christians at some point took a turn toward being "safe" from the influence of the world and from difficulties and pain. So much so, they successfully insulated themselves from a great deal of needed development through experiencing difficulty. Many Christians of my own generation were raised in a bubble (hiding from "the world") and have experienced so little true suffering that they really cannot relate to a suffering world. They are not resilient. They are not compassionate. They have little to no understanding of how to help suffering people find healing (if they even encounter such people in their sheltered lives). They remain shallow, underdeveloped, immature, and ineffective in the world, having no greater goals in life than to quietly raise their children in safety, marry them off as "pure" virgins with no actual relationship experience that could have helped them develop into a person capable of having a mature relationship, and then watch their own children do the same until they die. They will, of course, attend church, read their Bibles, and they may even engage with the Holy Spirit at times, though to little or no effect on the world around them.

I would like to state unequivocally that as Christians, we have no business being safe. We are called to be dangerous. We are called to establish Christ's dominion over the earth by tearing down the strongholds of darkness in our world. We are called to destroy the works of the evil one. We have no business hiding from the world, from the vulnerability of true intimacy, from exposing ourselves to situations where there may be danger. Our job is to enforce the rule of heaven in the realm of earth, in the face of all opposition if necessary. And make no mistake, there will be great opposition if we are acting as the people God created us to be. What will we do the first time we are faced with the rejection, hatred, and persecution of the world promised by Scripture (John 15) if we've never learned what to do with suffering? What will believers do when faced with the choice of denying Christ or suffering torture, torment, and death? How on earth will we claim to offer hope to the broken if we have no concept of healing ourselves because we have never allowed ourselves to be in situations where we could suffer pain?

The call of heaven is not, "Come escape from the world and just hold on until you reach heaven." It is, "Come learn who you are, grow into it, and storm the gates of hell." I'm not sure most Christians realize we are at war, and if they do, they do not seem to realize that war is violent. Training for war is often painful. Anyone with any experience in physical training can attest to bruises, sore muscles, burning lungs, and a host of other painful sensations while preparing for an athletic event or simply trying to be physically active and healthy. The things worth doing in life have a cost; they require us to not shrink back in the face of difficulty or pain, to set our faces like flint, keeping our eyes on the greater goal.

War is filled with pain. But until the enemy is finally defeated, we have no business pretending we don't need to know how to do battle. It is not a coincidence that Ephesians chapter 6 uses the "armor of God" to discuss preparedness in the Kingdom. The armor may be discussed allegorically, as many spiritual concepts are, but be assured, the war is not allegorical. This war is quite real in the spiritual realm, and though we in the Western world have not yet truly begun to experience it in the physical realm, you can be certain that it is coming. Our brothers and sisters in many nations around the world have lived in its reality for some time.

In addition to understanding the current war, in which we will be called to persevere in the midst of great suffering, Christians are called to have an eternal perspective. In comparison to eternity, the eighty or ninety years we have on this earth is a blip on the radar. Yet, it is an essential and foundational stage of our development, just like the infant learning to walk. One of my deepest longings, one that I pray for often, is that I will leave this life an adult, that I will have worked out the salvation of my soul with fear and trembling to the point that my soul has become used to feasting on steak and has left milk far behind.

Pain is necessary for growth. We even have a name for the pain often felt as our bodies stretch and add matter to themselves. "Growing pains," we call them. My long and lanky son has felt them often. He does not find them enjoyable, but the day his height surpassed his older sister was one of the happiest days of his life thus far. And the greater the tasks that his body is able to accomplish as he grows, the less his growing pains concern him. And so it works with our souls. Without exposure to difficulty, pain, and even suffering, we will not grow. We will remain infants, desperately looking for someone else to do the difficult things while God's army suffers from too few warriors.

And such pain is only available to us in this one, short span of years on this earth. I pray continuously that I will take advantage of every opportunity pain provides, that I will not waste the precious gift of temporary suffering, but instead use it to become the most mature and developed version of myself that God and I partnering together can achieve in one lifetime.

It may seem extreme to call suffering a gift. The Bible claims otherwise. In Matthew chapter 5, Jesus states clearly,

3 "Blessed are the poor in spirit,
for theirs is the kingdom of heaven.
4 Blessed are those who mourn,
for they will be comforted.
5 Blessed are the meek,
for they will inherit the earth.
6 Blessed are those who hunger and thirst for righteousness,
for they will be filled.
7 Blessed are the merciful,
for they will be shown mercy.
8 Blessed are the pure in heart,
for they will see God.
9 Blessed are the peacemakers,
for they will be called children of God.
10 Blessed are those who are persecuted because of righteousness,
for theirs is the kingdom of heaven.
11 "Blessed are you when people insult you, persecute you and falsely say all kinds of evil against you because of me.
12 Rejoice and be glad, because great is your reward in heaven, for in the same way they persecuted the prophets who were before you."

We are called blessed if we mourn, if we are poor in spirit, and if we are persecuted. We are told that great treasures await us in eternity because of these very experiences. It can seem like a distant concept, bearing little weight on our day-to-day lives, but we must keep eternity in mind. This short, foundational stage of our lives that takes place on this earth is minuscule in comparison to eternity. Yet, we earn eternal rewards here. It is only here where we have the opportunity to step out in faith because here we cannot see fully. Only here do we have the chance to worship God in the middle of trials that we fear might break us, because only here do we have such trials. On this earth alone is where we are provided the chance of maintaining hope in the face of anguish, because only here do we experience anguish. There is no need for faith or hope in heaven because we will have all things for which we have hoped, we will see all things for which we have had faith. Only in this life, here, now, are we given the chance to offer God the sacrifice of praise in the middle of desperate pain and unbearable grief.

I do not believe the Beatitudes listed above imply that suffering alone will result in our being blessed. There will be many people who have suffered greatly who do not ultimately choose to spend eternity with the One who could heal them. But I believe the Beatitudes imply that those who have suffered and sought and maintained loyalty and faithfulness to the Lord despite their pain will receive the reward promised for each of the types of suffering listed. It is those who staunchly refuse to impute the character of God with wrongdoing for their difficulties. Those who, like Job, fall down and worship their Creator in the midst of grief, loss, and inescapable agony of soul. I plan to be one of these. I hope you do as well.

CHAPTER 8

Brothers and sisters, stop thinking like children.
In regard to evil be infants, but in your thinking be adults.

—1 Corinthians 14:20

Again, I want to be clear that I do not subscribe to the belief that God creates our suffering. Other than some very narrow parameters to be discussed in subsequent chapters of this book, I do not think God orchestrates specific instances of suffering in our lives. I do not intentionally place barriers, difficulties, sorrow, or suffering in my children's path as they grow. I don't have to. I have no wish to see them suffer, and yet I know that each time I can help guide them through difficulties that arise from sources other than me, they are maturing. They are learning what love actually looks like and what it does not. They gain discernment—a gift desperately needed in today's world. They learn the difference between safe and unsafe people with whom to have relationships. They learn their own limitations and their own surprising strength. They learn forgiveness, compassion, and how to avoid causing pain to others whenever possible.

I also do not "allow" others to harm my children. If I see another person harming my child, I will put a stop to it immediately. I will not allow them to be mistreated so that they *learn lessons.* But I do then try to teach them the skills and wisdom they need in order to know how to respond when someone mistreats, betrays, or harms them because I know it will happen. I cannot walk around with them every moment to block every attempt by another human to hurt my children. I am not omnipresent, and I cannot control other people (that would violate their free will). And it is also because my goal for my children is maturity, that someday they will be adults, capable of navigating conflict, holding compassion for difficult people, speaking truth in love, while simultaneously not allowing themselves to be used or taken advantage of.

When my oldest daughter was freshly graduated from high school, she got her first "real" job working at a retail store. Several of her coworkers turned out to be rather unkind individuals. My daughter is naturally a happy, bubbly person, and her joy for life seemed to rub them the wrong way. They gossiped about her, told untrue stories about her work performance to her managers, and often refused to acknowledge her opinions or even her existence. Even one of her managers, whose romantic interest she had not returned, began to take part in the mistreatment and left her little avenue to try to address the situation with her bosses. It was a difficult circumstance, and she had to make decisions about how to handle it. Thankfully, she handled it with grace. She firmly, but kindly, set boundaries, processed her emotions about her coworkers' behaviors toward her in a healthy way, acknowledging and feeling them, then releasing them, and continued to be courteous and kind to her coworkers whenever she had the opportunity.

She did speak with me several times about the situation to get my perspective. I gave her my thoughts and then gave her the space she needed to make decisions about her own future.

What would have happened if, the first time she told me about her coworkers' treatment, I had stormed into the store, demanding to speak to the manager and the owner about how she was being treated? What if I had confronted her coworkers or her inappropriate manager? What if I had threatened legal action?

Several things may have happened and none of them beneficial to my daughter or anyone else. She would have lost a great deal of credibility among the people she worked with to whom she had been trying to display the love of God. I would have lost credibility in our community as unhinged, overprotective, and controlling. She would have lost a great opportunity to learn about loving difficult people, setting boundaries to protect herself, and recognizing when an environment is a place we are meant to remain and spread light or when it's a place we need to leave behind. I would have been laughed out of the store because she was a legal adult. If she chose not to pursue legal action, there is not one thing I could have done to sue the store, the manager, or anyone else involved. And we sometimes seem to forget that there are laws in the spirit just like there are laws in the natural world.

You see, we have all these questions about God "allowing" suffering, questions that we instinctively know the answer to in our day-to-day lives. I know very few people who would have found such actions on my part to be appropriate or productive. Even so, we are driven to a crisis of faith at times because God doesn't act in quite that way. I didn't "allow" my daughter to suffer these difficulties. They came from a source that, even if I'd had the ability to control, would have been inappropriate for me to control. Instead, my position of relationship with her allowed me to give her some guidance (though she didn't need much) about making decisions that would turn out for her good. She benefitted, and no one's free will was violated. This was able to happen because I'd already spent time teaching her about boundaries, forgiveness, and conflict in age-appropriate contexts.

Somehow, we end up with the idea that we should be the ones determining in which situations God *should* have intervened and thus violated someone else's free will on our behalf. I doubt we would have the same thoughts if it was our free will He was violating.

My hope for my children is not that they never know pain or difficulty. I hate when they do. I hate to see them suffering. But my goal for them is much greater. It is that they will become mature individuals, capable of making a greater impact on the world than I ever have and to build the type of resiliency that is absolutely vital to a true and vibrant faith—faith that doesn't waiver because something painful touched their lives, faith able to sustain a belief in God's goodness in the worst of circumstances (which the Bible tells us are coming).

God's goal for our lives isn't to never experience pain. His goal for us is infinitely higher than this. He desires that we will continuously choose to expend more and more of our free will loving and honoring Him and His people as we engage in the process of what old theologians used to call sanctification, the "being saved" that we're in this life to accomplish. That way, when the final showdown between good and evil takes place, we are not only firmly found on the side of good, but we actually have some power, some strength, some stamina to tear down the gates of hell and send evil fleeing in terror.

Free Will

CHAPTER 9

...then choose for yourselves this day whom you will serve...
—Joshua 24:15

There's another concept connected very closely to incidental suffering during the process of maturing: the concept of free will. Free will has been discussed by innumerable theologians throughout the ages, so you may not find anything unexpected in these pages. However, God gave me a deeper revelation of the part that free will plays in pain and suffering in the course of my journey to understand my own life experiences, and I believe some may find it helpful.

Growing up in church, I always understood free will to mean that God allows us to choose whether or not we will follow Him and to choose what actions we take in our lifetimes. This is true, but it is a basic and incomplete understanding.

I never really felt that I understood why free will was so necessary to our existence. It never felt like a fully adequate explanation of the horrors that one human can perpetrate against another. When I began to understand some of God's motives for how He designed creation, I was shocked.

First and foremost is His reason for creating humanity. Why did God make us? Some part of me had long suspected that it was for the same reason my mother chose to have children. He was looking for people to control and hold to an impossible standard of perfection that no one could meet. Then, He could feel justified in punishing them for nothing more than His own amusement.

What I came to realize, however, was that God created people for the same reason that most adults (who were not my parents) choose to have children. He wanted a family. He didn't need one. The absolute fullness of love and connection was already present among the members of the Trinity. But what do you do when you are utterly overflowing with love? You find people to give it to! He created us in order to enlarge His family, to spend all of eternity loving, enjoying, teaching, and discovering with us. We are His delight. We were the prize set before Jesus for which He endured the cross. The most loving and devoted earthly parent can barely brush the edges of the love that God has for us. The primary purpose for which we were created is to be loved, perfectly and unconditionally.

Love, however, requires free will. In fact, I am convinced that a person's ability to love is directly and proportionally tied to their ability to allow the person they love to exercise their free will. If, in order for your spouse or friend to spend time with you, you had to inject them with a drug that made them complacent and controllable, how loved would you feel after? Love flourishes in freedom. Love dies under the influence of control.

Some people find it arousing when their partners display a certain level of possessiveness over them, not wanting them to speak to members of the opposite sex, keeping track of where they go and to whom they send messages. But this obsessive, dysfunctional control is a poor substitute for actual love, which instead says, "I choose you, will you choose me?" and then trusts what the other person has told them. Does this freedom open the potential for betrayal and pain? Of course it does. Nearly all things worth having require some level of risk. You can be certain, however, that betrayal and pain are nearly guaranteed if you do not give your partner the freedom to choose you or not to.

Churches are filled with parents of "prodigal" children, pleading for prayer each week, hoping their child "returns to the Lord." What I am about to say does not apply equally to every situation of the prodigal children of Christian parents. However, many of these children cannot "return" to the Lord because the Lord was never displayed to them by their parents in the first place. Sadly, the church has a longstanding history of parents who guilt, shame, manipulate, bully, and control their children into behavior modification. These children often grow up with such a warped view of God that they want nothing to do with the church or God Himself. They cannot be blamed for this perspective. The blame lies squarely on the shoulders of their parents who made them believe that God wanted to control them into obedience instead of setting them free with the tools needed to thrive. This was the primary goal of "purity culture," popular in evangelical Christianity in the 1990s and early 2000s, to control Christian young people into remaining virgins until marriage through tactics of fear and shame (rather than leading them with love into a healthy understanding of the roles of covenant and intimacy in their lives).

But you see, humans were not designed to be controlled. They were designed to be loved, which is the antithesis of control. Possessiveness in romantic relationships is an utterly wasted emotion, as are all possessive actions. It is impossible for you to force someone to remain faithful to you. Every attempt will nearly guarantee the demise of your relationship. Either the person will choose you continuously or they will not. It is entirely up to them. No amount of freedom will cause them to betray you if it is not in their heart to do so. They will choose to set their own appropriate boundaries to ensure their faithfulness, or they will not. No amount of tracking their movements and determining who they can speak to will keep them from being unfaithful if it is in their heart to be so. And you are more likely to push a partner into unfaithfulness with excessive control than if you had allowed them to make choices of their own free will, creating the very scenario that so terrified you.

In the same way, attempts to control children into certain behaviors will nearly always result in them rebelling, becoming bitter and angry, and potentially severing any meaningful relationship with their parents, or at least their parents' faith. These children are not prodigals in the biblical sense of the word. In the biblical account of the prodigal son, the father made no attempt to control or even convince his son to remain at home and behave. When the son requested to receive his inheritance before the established time, he was given it, regardless of the pain a father would have felt in that situation. There was no guilt, no manipulation, no attempt to force a particular outcome. Because of this, when this son's life fell to pieces, he knew where he needed to go to find relief and assistance. He knew where he could find safety and a new path forward.

All of the "prodigal" children raised in churches by controlling, overbearing parents are not prodigals at all; they do not know the love that their Father has for them or the goodness waiting in His house. They are not prodigals. They are purely and simply *unsaved*. Only, as William Paul Young would say, they have much further to go in their journey to salvation than the typical unsaved individual because they have to *unlearn* the damaging representations they were taught about God before they can learn the truth about Him. This is the result of control in place of love. Control leads to death, whereas freedom leads to life. The love of God is so immense that He gives us absolute freedom to choose.

Imagine if we could show a love like this, a love that not only allowed but absolutely demanded the honoring of the free will of those we loved. The world would be upended. We must ask, who is our father? Is it God, truly? Or like the Pharisees, is it the devil, the author of control? It is time for the church to stop lying to the world about who God is by clinging to our desperate need for control and rejecting the ways of our King. Jesus did not establish His church to take dominion over people. He established his church to take dominion over darkness.

Let's start with tearing down the stronghold of control in our own structures. Even if no one but believers began to lay down their need for control and instead promote each other's freedom of choice, the world would never be the same. Don't you think it's time for us to act toward one another as God has acted toward us? I suspect that this would be a bride ready for the arrival of her Husband.

CHAPTER 10

I tell you that in the same way there will be more rejoicing in heaven over one sinner who repents than over ninety-nine righteous persons who do not need to repent.

—Luke 15:7

I hope it is clear how free will is absolutely essential in relationship. There can be no relationship without it. God knew, in order to have the family He so desired, He would have to create us with the ability to choose Him or not to. So very many people do not. His heart is broken by each and every one. But as I mentioned, the degree of freedom indicates the degree of love that exists in a relationship. God's love for us is so vast, so unimaginably all-encompassing, that He will allow us to walk right into hell if we so choose. If people decide they do not want God in their lives, then there is only one place in existence where God is not. It was not created for humans, it was created for Satan and his ilk, but humans have the freedom to choose to go there if they desire an existence without God.

I would go so far as to suggest that the vast majority of suffering in this world is the result of one person's attempt to violate another person's free will. All attempts at control are violations of someone's free will. Overt examples such as violence, rape, abuse, and murder are obvious examples of violations of individuals' free will. But even more subtle forms of control such as emotional manipulation are insidious violations of the free will of others.

So, the question then becomes, if we were required to have free will in order to partake in a relationship based on love, does it mean free will has to result in suffering?

In *The Problem of Pain*, C.S. Lewis makes the claim that in any situation where free will exists, inevitably a choice will be made in opposition to established expectations or precepts. It is the nature of free will that it must be used. No human has ever had a perfectly obedient child. We would all be concerned if we did. As tiresome as certain stages of development can be in our children when they feel the need to definitively establish their independence and autonomy, we would all be concerned parents if they never went through those stages of pushing boundaries. That's the nature of free-willed individuals.

Some might attribute this to the sin nature. I strongly believe that it is designed by God. If He was looking for children who would be perfectly obedient robots from day one, he would have done away with the idea of free will altogether. But I believe that, as much as the entrance of sin into the world broke His heart, along with the subsequent suffering sin has caused, God actually wants children who are certain to the very depths of their souls that He is what they want and nothing else. And for many people, what ultimately drives them to this place of understanding is the utter failure of every other attempt to satisfy the deepest longings of their own souls. They come to the point where they are certain beyond a shadow of a doubt that only He can fill all spaces within them, making them whole.

This may be theologically stretching for some, but it appears likely that the prodigal son loved and appreciated his father deeply after his return, with a new depth of humility and understanding. This humility and appreciation of his father are evident in the story. His brother, on the other hand, remained entitled, bitter, and jealous, never having come to the same understanding of all his father had done for him. Instead, the older brother focused on all that he had done for his father.

I have sometimes felt bothered by the notion that heaven rejoices over one lost sinner who comes to repentance more than ninety-nine who did not need to. But could it be partly because the choice of the one who returned was filled to the brim with the understanding of what it really was that was offered to him by his Creator? This one is filled with a depth of gratitude and love that simply cannot be achieved without having made other choices first and found them insufficient and empty. Didn't Jesus Himself say in Luke chapter 7 that the person who has been forgiven much loves much? Scripture seems to support the notion that it's better to return to our Father from a place of distance and separation than to have never left in the first place. How can it not be when we return with a desire for His heart that we never would have developed in a thousand years without having experienced life without Him?

In the United States, there are a number of regional areas home to vast Amish communities. The Amish are very separated from the rest of society. They have their own farms that do not use electricity. They wear only certain types of clothing and only own horses and buggies for transportation. They have intentionally kept themselves separate from "the English" (the rest of us) for many generations. There is no intermarriage, no intimate friendships, no social connections. They are a wholly separate people. I do not agree with a great deal of their theology and some of their practices, but many Amish communities do have a rite of passage I find to be an excellent example of the concept I am trying to illustrate.

The time known as Rumspringa happens when an Amish child becomes a late teen. During this time, they allow, or in some cases, compel, their older teens to go out and experience what the world has to offer. This is sometimes referred to as "sowing their wild oats." They are free to try all of the activities that have long been restricted in their lives, and, when they are ready, to make a decision based on the information they learned from their Rumspringa. That decision is to either leave the Amish community to become "English," if they have found the "English" world to satisfy them to a greater extent than the one in which they were raised, or to return to their community and their family and remain Amish for the remainder of their lives. The catch is, if they choose the "English" world, they are shunned from their Amish community. They become "English" in all senses of the word. They are outsiders, no longer allowed to have intimate relationships or community with all the people they formerly knew. You may well guess that, though many find the freedoms and excitements of the English world intriguing, the vast majority of Amish teens who go through Rumspringa return to their communities in the end, unwilling to permanently give up the people they love, the way of life they know. And they are typically satisfied with their decision, having learned to appreciate what home offered them in comparison to the relative disconnection and distraction of the world. Most of them, it appears, live out the rest of their lives no longer thinking about what they might have missed by being Amish, but feel settled in their choice, content in their decision.

More and more I have come to believe that humanity's return to God from a state of sin and death (rather than being born into perfection as Adam and Eve were) is a great advantage to us.

CHAPTER 11

For he chose us in him before the creation of the world
to be holy and blameless in his sight.

—Ephesians 1:4

I have begun to touch on a concept that long puzzled me until God gave me greater revelation on it. I grew up being taught that the Garden of Eden was God's original intent for humanity, and Adam and Eve, for lack of a better term, screwed it up for all of us. So, God was required to quickly conference with Jesus to develop an alternate plan for humanity, which was salvation through the work of Christ on the cross. It was not, perhaps, said in exactly those terms, but that was the general idea conveyed. But as I began to understand more about this topic, I had a growing sense that we were, somehow, inexplicably better off in our current position than Adam and Eve had been. After all, they had it all—deeply connected, ongoing intimate relationship with God, animals who didn't view them as a potential meal, no sickness, no death—but that only left the possibility of going downward. There was no place to which they could climb up from there. They had a choice, a method by which to exercise their free will, but it could only go one direction, and upward was not it. We, however, start life utterly disconnected from our Maker, corrupted in soul, dying in body, facing a lifetime of one painful experience after another. When we exercise our free will, there are a myriad of options and addictions that can worsen the damaged state in which we already find ourselves. But there is also the possibility of using free will to return to the status and position with our Father that He always intended us to hold. We can have both: exercise our free will *and* be in loving connection with our Creator. Adam and Eve, in effect, could only have one or the other.

But I came to understand that it went even deeper than this. You see, if C.S. Lewis is to be believed (and I agree wholeheartedly with him), then someone would have eventually eaten the forbidden fruit. In a world of free-willed beings, if it wasn't Adam and Eve, it would have been one of their children. It would have been highly unlikely that the infraction would have been delayed until their grandchildren's generation. The nature of free will would not have allowed it. And so, no matter how long it took, there would always have been the fall of humanity just waiting to happen. As long as God was determined to give humankind an option other than Himself in order to preserve their free will, someone would have taken it. Death, sin, and suffering were inevitable. Even if it had somehow taken thousands of years before someone ate from the Tree of the Knowledge of Good and Evil, looming in the atmosphere the entirety of that time would have been the possibility of our separation from God. And I do not believe this was God's plan for our eternity. I believe His plan for our eternity was to spend forever enjoying His love and His presence without any possibility of it being taken from us.

But how could He accomplish this while preserving our free will? Exactly as He did, as it turns out. You see, we are not living in God's hastily constructed plan B for reality. This is it. This is plan A. Jesus was the Lamb that was slain before the foundations of the world (Rev. 13:8). Do we think that if there was another, better, way that an omniscient, omnipresent, omnipotent God would not have chosen it?

You see, we are born into sin, already separated from the Lover of our souls, the Sustainer of our being. We are desperate, disconnected, dying. We didn't have to choose sin and death. It was handed to us—an inheritance from our forefathers back to Adam. Is it enjoyable or pleasant for anyone? No, we have all experienced suffering in one form or another. And yet, we find ourselves in a unique position. We now have the option of choosing God because we've experienced life without Him. Adam and Eve did not have this choice. We don't have to have the option to choose separation from God. We are already separated. The choice now before us is not "Should I choose death?" but "Should I choose the Source of Life?" The exercise of our free will no longer only offers distance from Him, but the possibility of indescribable oneness.

And once we have made the choice to believe in Christ and the work He accomplished in defeating sin and death on the cross, once we have given the Lord permission to be the ruler of our lives, our choice has been made. Our free will has been honored. When we enter eternity, He no longer has to offer us the option of choosing something other than Him. We have already exercised our free will to choose—choosing Him. We are free to live as God always desired, with Him forever without the possibility of sin or death taking that from us.

The book of Revelation informs us that the Tree of Life will be present on the new earth after Jesus has finally and permanently defeated the devil and removed him from the world. The other tree from Eden, however, is nowhere to be seen in this accounting of our future. We already have the knowledge of good and evil, and in heaven we have chosen the good. At that time, it will never be taken from us again.

And so, I once again make the suggestion that we are in a much more desirable position than Adam and Eve were. God Himself not only knew that this would be the course human history would take, but He knew it was the best, and in fact, the only course it could follow in order for true and real love to win the day—for both free will and absolute immunity to destruction to exist simultaneously in His family for all eternity.

CHAPTER 12

God opposes the proud
but shows favor to the humble.

—James 4:6

As a final thought on free will, a school of thought has developed that seems to claim God never causes or allows us to experience suffering. I find this school of thought to be well-intentioned, but incorrect. Scripture makes it clear that God may cause or allow suffering in a person's life in what we might call a last-ditch effort to turn them from a path of their own destruction. This is the loving discipline of God, but I believe I can confidently say it's never His first choice. I have, like David, sometimes found myself frustrated over the number of chances that God, in fact, gives people who continue to choose evil. Before I came to a place of full forgiveness of my parents, I was, frankly, irritated with God for not smiting them for the years of torment they inflicted upon me. They did not change, they appeared to have no desire to change, and still, to this day, appear to be absent any desire to alter course. But as we know, God is slow to anger, abounding in love. He gives us chance after chance to see the error of our ways, turn back, repent, and choose Him once more. And so, it is not so often as we might hope that He smites the people who have wronged us.

Many people have questioned why God does not at least intervene to prevent horrible things from happening to innocent people. I will tell you a difficult truth. God loves the perpetrators of harm equally as much as He loves the victims. He does *not* for one moment approve of their harmful actions, take their "side" in abusive situations, or ask us to gloss over what they have done in the name of "forgiveness." Please understand me. His heart is wrenched over every moment of pain you have suffered at the hands of another person or because of circumstances outside your control. But we must remember that love and freedom go hand-in-hand. God would not remove the free will of the perpetrators of harm any more than He would take away yours; He has the exact same level of intense, overflowing love for them as He has for you. He desires their healing and wholeness as He desires yours.

Believe me, I know deeply how difficult it can be to swallow such a concept as a victim of life-shattering abuse. Hopefully, later chapters of this book will shed some light on how I came to not only forgive but to have an intense love of my own for the people who did everything in their power to destroy my soul. But He is slow to anger, abounding in love, giving second, third, fourth, and more chances to return to Him.

However, I do believe there comes a point where a person's heart is so hardened, so wholly against all things righteous and of God that God will intervene, causing or allowing suffering. He did so with Paul on the road to Damascus, blinding and terrifying him (Acts 9).

In 2 Chronicles 33, we can read the account of Manasseh, king of Judah. The first portion of this chapter details the many violations against God's laws in which Manasseh participated, including the murder of his own children. He was on a path of destruction not only for himself but was happily leading the nation of Israel down the same road. As we will read, God attempted to turn Manasseh back from his wicked ways, but he and the people of Israel would not listen. Verses 10–13:

"The Lord spoke to Manasseh and his people, but they paid no attention. So the Lord brought against them the army commanders of the king of Assyria, who took Manasseh prisoner, put a hook in his nose, bound him with bronze shackles and took him to Babylon. In his distress he sought the favor of the Lord his God and humbled himself greatly before the God of his ancestors. And when he prayed to him, the Lord was moved by his entreaty and listened to his plea; so he brought him back to Jerusalem and to his kingdom. Then Manasseh knew that the Lord is God."

It is clear in this account that it was Manasseh's experience of suffering, humiliation, and captivity that ultimately turned his heart toward God. It is equally as clear that God initiated these instances of suffering in his life for just this purpose. I fully believe that we often suffer the natural consequences of our actions which can often be painful. But in this case, and in many similar cases, particularly concerning Old Testament kings of Israel and Judah, the Bible makes it perfectly clear the suffering is initiated by God.

It was not His desire or His first choice. He attempted other means by which to reach Manasseh, as He did with many other kings throughout the Old Testament, as I believe He still does with individuals today. It was successful in the case of Manasseh. It was not always successful with other leaders of Israel, unfortunately, and it is not always successful when God makes a final attempt to turn hearts toward Him today through the initiation of suffering. But when this method is used by the Lord, we can be certain that it was the only option left to Him. We can be certain that He made every attempt through every other means to reach those who ultimately experience such harsh discipline.

Even in situations where God initiates or allows disaster or difficulty to interrupt the actions of those whose hearts are bent on evil, I believe His intent is still to draw those individuals to Himself. He knows drastic measures are the only chance left that they will seek Him. We see this on many occasions in the Old Testament, not only with individuals but with the nation of Israel. Whenever Israel became so corrupt, so filled with evil that they would not return to Him on their own, He would lift his blanket of protection from them and allow, and sometimes initiate, disaster against them. In their hardened condition, He knew this was the only tool left available to attempt to bring them back to His love and protection. Some of Israel's difficulties were brought on themselves as natural consequences of their own actions. But often it was the final attempt by a loving Father to discipline His children away from death and toward life. The book of Judges appears to be one long saga of Israel ping-ponging back and forth between utter corruption and humble repentance after oppression and captivity.

There is more biblical precedent for God placing Himself in opposition to the hard-hearted and stiff-necked than many people in the modern church would find comfortable or easy to accept. The Bible clearly states that God "opposes the proud" (James 4:6). It does not say He ignores them, takes a step back, and allows the chips to fall where they may. Oppose is not a passive verb, the implication being that He is *actively* against them. In Acts 13, we see Paul, after a sorcerer has attempted to interfere with the proconsul of Cyprus hearing or receiving the Gospel, tell the man that God "opposes him," after which he immediately becomes blind. It is clear from this story that God's opposition carries with it actual, real consequences and meaningful difficulty. It is not a powerless statement. And this was in the New Testament—post-resurrection.

We have a strange idea in the twenty-first-century church that God does not set Himself against people. I would argue that He is the same yesterday, today, and forever. The difference between the Old and New Testaments of the Bible is a change in the possibility of salvation and relationship with God. We now have an actual choice to receive the salvation and abundant life He always desired for us to have. It is the opening of a new pathway forward for us into eternity with the Lord and the ability to effectively bring eternity into this realm here and now. It is a change in available solutions. But it is not a change in the character of God, and it is not a change in the character of humanity.

Human beings still become so self-impressed, so eaten up with pride and self-importance, so corrupt in heart, that the only possibility of turning them back to the Lord is for them to experience great loss—loss of power, position, reputation, importance, money, people, whatever it may be in which they had found their security and identity to their own detriment. I have a strong suspicion that when the Holy Spirit reveals to us an effective solution for the healing of those with narcissistic personality disorder, it will involve a great deal of loss and suffering on their part—loss of everything upon which they had built their false selves, their houses of cards. Again, I do not believe this is God's first choice, and it is certainly not something to expect as the result of mistakes or even strongholds of sin in our lives. It is literally those who oppose God, in the truest sense of the word, whom He opposes.

The fact that we see God inflicting suffering on stubborn, hard-hearted people in the Bible is likely what has led to the poor theology permeating Evangelical Christianity, which says God inflicts us with suffering to teach us lessons. I want to be as clear as humanly possible on this subject. I am convinced that no matter what level of sin, destruction, stronghold, or addiction you are living in, if there is the smallest hint of a whisper of a genuine thought in your mind that you wish to be healed, set free, in better relationship with God, then you are not the person to whom God sets Himself in opposition. The Bible is clear that His kindness brings us to repentance (Romans 2:4). I am absolutely convinced that the loving-kindness of God only manifests itself as intentional suffering and opposition in the case of individuals (or nations) who have long ago stopped maintaining any concern about their own spiritual and eternal standing. Such difficulties are the only force that will act as a catalyst for a possible change of course. If you are still on a journey of healing, freedom, and growth (even if you find yourself falling into the same old pattern of sin and brokenness over and over again), you needn't worry about finding God in opposition to you any time in the near future. It is when the journey has stopped and there is arrogant refusal to self-examine, operate in humility, or in any way move toward God that His discipline may start. However, it may not initially be perceived as kindness by those experiencing it.

I would like to make it clear that in these situations, the Lord did not violate the free will of these individuals. He never removed their ability to choose idolatry, evil, and death. He simply caused them to experience some of the harsher possible consequences of these choices. There are times when He acts in this way now as well. Many a hardened criminal has found salvation in a prison cell when his death-dealing ways have finally caught up to him. And yet there are still some who refuse to be chastised, no matter how painful or difficult their situations become. I am thoroughly convinced that the swath of Christian leaders who have been exposed for predatory sins against others in recent times, in many cases, has taken place because these leaders absolutely refused to address their areas of sin stronghold in private. I do not believe that public exposure is God's first choice to correct leaders who are in bondage to sin. But I do believe there are many cases where the person has become so insulated from correction and accountability that they have ceased to be concerned about their own actions and how others might be affected by them. In many cases, a hardness of heart toward their own condition left God with little choice in correcting them but to use something very painful and public.

One night as I was speaking with Jesus about forgiveness of my ex-husband for a decade of abuse, he showed me a picture of the state of the man. He was a small boy, being dragged by a chain behind a fast-moving cart. He became bloody and beaten, but eventually got free of the cart. He never got free of the chain, however. He remained a little boy, draped in the links of dark, rusty metal, arms folded across his chest. Every now and then, Jesus would approach the boy and ask if he wanted freedom. He would huff and turn his back on Jesus, satisfied to stay an angry child for the remainder of his life. I was struggling with forgiveness at the time and felt that this man was nothing more than a pathetic excuse for a human being. This image of him did not initially sway me to change my opinion.

Sometime later when I was speaking with the Lord again on the same topic, he explained to me that "He is to be pitied above all other types of people because he is clinging desperately to his own destruction."

There will be those who refuse the call of the Lord despite even the harsh disciplinary measures that the Lord, in love, takes in an attempt to save them. But even they do not deserve our hatred or disdain. They deserve our pity. They are like Gollum in the *Lord of the Rings*, sinking slowly into a volcano filled with lava, still clinging desperately to the thing that has destroyed him and will ultimately kill him. And although sad, they have been given the free will to make that decision.

There will be many more such people the nearer we come to the end of this age. Many will become so hardened that they will make an irreversible decision: taking the mark of the beast (in whatever form that takes). Doing so, they reject the kingship of their own Creator, instead clinging to the beast that plans their destruction. They will exercise their free will to utterly spurn the One who loves them, and He will allow them to do it. But I am convinced that until each person's final moment of decision, whether that is death or, as we near the end of all things, the decision to take the mark of the beast, the Lord will continue to use every means available to Him to turn hearts back to Himself, back to the source of healing and life. For many, this will mean a gentle touch, the kind hand of the Father. For others, it will entail difficulty and suffering, initiated by that same loving Father.

Types of Suffering

(And How to Rightly Understand Them)

CHAPTER 13

God is our refuge and strength,
an ever-present help in trouble.

—Psalm 46:1

In a previous chapter, I discussed experiencing suffering as a part of our growth and maturity. I would like to clarify that God can use all types of suffering to further our growth, and He delights in turning our pain into something to be used for our good. But I'd like to now address the fact that there are different types of suffering.

There is a type of suffering that, by its very nature, tends to cause growth in us. People who experience this type of suffering are likely to grow from it whether they know the Lord or not. This type of suffering is that of natural consequences. If we get our first job and excitedly spend every paycheck we make on new gadgets and luxuries, but then our phone or electricity gets disconnected because we did not pay the bill, we are likely to learn to prioritize better how we spend our money. If we are driving our car too fast on ice-covered roads and wreck as a result, we are likely to drive a bit more cautiously the next time road conditions are not ideal. We grow quickly and easily from natural consequences without having to put too much work or thought into the process. However, if we know the Lord, our growth and maturity from our own mistakes are likely to accelerate much more quickly than we would without Him.

It may have been the hypervigilance from growing up immersed in abuse, or it may have been the hyperfocus provided to me by an autistic brain, but I have always been a quick learner from natural consequences. With few (but stark) areas of exception, I have rarely made the same mistake twice in my life, because I always remembered those mistakes. If I incorrectly answered a test question in school, I would remember the correct information for years beyond what I answered correctly on that same test. Mistakes are a very effective way to grow and mature, as long as we desire to do so.

Next, there is a type of suffering that is incidental. We live in a world of death, and we come across difficult things through no fault of our own or of the people in our lives. An animal in the road that causes us to wreck our vehicle, an economic crash that causes us to lose our life savings, or a sickness picked up from contact with a friend. These difficulties can tempt us to spiral into a place of fear and control. We can't predict the economy, so we develop a poverty mentality, hoarding our money and resources. We can't control when an animal might be in the road, so we drive irrationally slowly or choose not to drive anymore at all. We cannot predict illnesses, so we begin to obsessively wash our hands and avoid close contact with anyone who may have been exposed to sickness. On the extreme end of negative responses to this type of unpredictable suffering, we find people with severe anxiety, refusing to leave their homes for fear of car accidents, germs, or people thinking poorly of them, living in absolute bondage to fear. Most do not reach this level of slavery to fear, but fear is a tempting response to an unpredictable world whether we're a believer or not.

People who have either grown up in stable, loving homes or have developed the skills necessary to mentally and emotionally process unpredictability will often use this type of suffering to assist in their growth. They will learn how to successfully battle fear, use wisdom, lean on their loved ones, and develop the resiliency needed to spur themselves on to rebuild the things they've lost, finding new paths to achieve their dreams. They will grieve what needs to be grieved, let go of what must be released, and step into the next chapter of life with at least some measure of hope for the future. Sadly, such people are few and far between. There are, by far, more people who've never known what it means to recover from difficulty or heal from suffering than those who have. They never had the foundation or gained the tools to know how to respond when life does not go in the direction they planned, when they have worked hard for something and the return for their work is insufficient or even disastrous.

In my early twenties, I was a college student with all sorts of dreams for my future. My goal was to have a career in the field of International Intelligence. I hoped to work for the U.S. government in anti-terrorism or other espionage-based positions. Consequently, I graduated high school as the valedictorian of my class, maintained a high GPA in college, and earned degrees in psychology and criminology. I took every necessary step to achieve this goal. I was highly athletic, motivated, and determined. I received academic awards, built an impressive resume, and purchased book after book on the career field of intelligence. There was just one notable difficulty.

I had contracted the mononucleosis virus in college. For most people, this virus causes a terrible sore throat, exhaustion, and swollen glands for a few weeks—a miserable length of time by all accounts for such a sickness. But then their immune system pulls itself together and fights the thing off, and they return to normal health and life. Mine, however, did not. My immune system did not defeat the virus; it was defeated by it. I developed a chronic case of mononucleosis, commonly known as Chronic Fatigue Syndrome. My glands were always painfully swollen, my throat sore, my head throbbing. My body was always exhausted, and yet the condition itself prevented sleep. If I even attempted what I would have once considered a laughably easy level of exercise, the symptoms of my disease became so unbearable that I could not remove myself from the couch for days at a time.

Within a few short years of this, and while I was still living in this condition, I developed an autoimmune disorder that caused my body to attack nearly all of its systems when I consumed anything other than plain meat, eggs, and green vegetables. This lasted for years. Because of this diet, I also developed gout, a painful condition that gave me the sensation of being stabbed in the bottom of my feet with a rack of knives every time I took a step. Because of even further dietary restrictions to which I was forced to adhere in order to be able to walk, I developed a condition in my bladder called cystitis, where the lining was stripped away, leaving me with the sensation that I desperately needed to use the bathroom every moment of every day. There were other health conditions that developed beyond those listed here, but these are the most notable.

Every dream I had fell to pieces by the roadside. I couldn't even maintain a normal job, let alone the career I had spent years dreaming of. As you may imagine based on my childhood, I had no resiliency, no ability to believe that the future would ever be better than the present. No one had ever looked out for or protected me. The only person who had ever attempted to do anything for my benefit was *me*. And now I had lost the ability to do almost anything at all. I still tried. Sometimes I pushed myself so hard that I would collapse. Sometimes I just walked on the knives because I needed groceries. But ultimately, I came to the realization that the only person who had ever taken care of me could no longer do so.

The devastation I felt can hardly be overstated. I was destroyed. I had done everything I knew to do to pull myself up by my bootstraps, out of the misery of my past, and make something of my life, only to be driven off a cliff by circumstances over which I had zero control. It could not be borne.

I was broken. And I believed God hated me. I had done everything right, and He had taken every bit of it from me.

Then, one night I had a dream. I knew it was from God. He'd been speaking to me in my dreams since I was a teenager when I had desperately asked Him to give me a sign of His existence.

In this dream, I stopped by the side of the road to check on a cornfield that I had planted. When I stood in front of the field looking at the long stretch of ground, I saw tall, vibrant green corn stalks, and growing on them were the most enormous ears of corn I had ever seen. I knew that the best kind of sweet corn is what's known as bi-colored corn. It has both yellow and white kernels on the ear. I knew this was the variety of corn I had planted—only the best—but this was not the corn that had grown in my field. What I saw on these bizarrely large ears of corn were all yellow kernels. One after another I looked at the ears and saw only yellow. Yellow everywhere. I held one giant ear of corn in my arms like a baby and wept bitterly over what was not there. It seemed to matter little that one single ear of corn I had planted was big enough to feed a family, kernels so full it was practically bursting in my arms. Even so, it was not what I had planted, not what I wanted.

Then, I looked more closely at the ear and noticed yet another imperfection. On normal ears of corn there tend to be a few rows of shriveled, underdeveloped kernels near the top of the ear that have not yet grown to full maturity. This was not the case with mine. The tops of my ears of corn were full and ready to burst. At the base of the ear, however, where it had been connected to the stalk, there were multiple rows of these shrunken, undersized kernels. I was dissatisfied. I had expected perfection. This was not it. I wept in anguish once again. This was my life.

I knew immediately that this dream was about my life, but it took me quite a long time to realize the message in it. The base of my life, my foundation, the place from which I grew, was a shriveled place of immaturity and death. And yet, despite that, God would build from that foundation of suffering a life so full, so bursting with abundance that it would replace three or four "normal" lives worth of fruit. He had no intention of allowing the suffering and brokenness I had experienced in early life to prevent me from having over and above anything I had planned or imagined in my life, even if it did not look the way I expected it to.

And to be honest, looking back, I am not thankful for illness, but I am so thankful that I was prevented from following my dream to completion. You see, I am tenacious. I don't give up easily. I would have followed that dream through to the end until I had reached it or died trying. And it would have been the worst thing that could have happened to me. At the time, I believed it was the best possible career for me because of how my life had developed. I had plenty of acquaintances, but few friends, certainly none that I would have been devastated to leave behind. I had no intention of developing close and intimate relationships with anyone in my life, but at the same time, I craved purpose, meaning, and frankly, a challenge. Having learned to live my entire life from a state of performance, I could have and would have happily worked the sixty or so hours per week averaged by most intelligence agents, if not more, with no worries about family or connections. I would have happily exchanged my true identity for one or many others in the course of gathering intelligence. I did not see the death in such a life—only the relief of isolation and the draw of doing something for a purpose higher than myself. I had no idea that what God had in mind for me was, in fact, relief *from* isolation and a purpose so high that it was outside the scope of my imagination at that time.

Healthwise, I function on a relatively normal level these days. Some of my health conditions are being successfully treated with medical interventions, some have been supernaturally healed directly by the Lord Himself, and at least one was healed simply by becoming pregnant with my first biological child.

I did know the Lord, but I was by no means living in freedom at the time in my life when my health struggles began. The layers of lies I had to unlearn about God and about myself were staggering. Yet, He still used my low level of relational maturity with Him to give me some kind of hope for my future.

Is it possible to learn to use this unpredictable, seemingly random type of suffering for our own growth and maturity without Him? It is not as likely, but it can happen. We can learn skills that lead to resiliency and train our minds and brains into healthier ways of functioning. However, it will never carry the depth of truth, healing, and eternal value that the same growth would carry with God at the center and in the working. We may become more mature, but we will not become any more aware of our true identity. We will not develop the faith to depend upon the goodness of God in the midst of unpredictability and insecurity. There are depths of growth, necessary depths, that are only available to us through relationship with the One who orders the stars while our worlds collapse around us.

I have learned more about God's goodness through suffering than I possibly could have absent its presence, but only because of *His* Presence in my life simultaneously. God does not orchestrate our suffering, but

He is thrilled to take it and form it into something that will build us instead of break us. And if we can relinquish our hold on fear and let Him do it, there is no limit to what He can accomplish in and through us.

CHAPTER 14

But I tell you, love your enemies and pray
for those who persecute you…
—Matthew 5:44

Another type of suffering that I would like to discuss is suffering that's perpetrated against us by others. Now of course, within this category, there is pain that we experience by the actions of others that unintentionally results in our hurt. Even the most loving person is likely to accidentally cause you pain at some point in your relationship with them. But if the relationship is healthy, the hurt can be openly discussed, processed, and healed without the relationship or the people involved suffering any long-term ill effects. It is a normal occurrence in even the healthiest relationships and is nothing to be feared or avoided. This is not the type of suffering to which I am referring here.

The type of suffering I would like to address now is that which is perpetrated against us by others, either as a byproduct of their own brokenness or intentionally and malevolently. This suffering is completely unnecessary and is not the result of any choices we've made or any unpredictable or unexpected circumstances. It is an exercise of the free will of another human against us. It cuts deep and grips us violently. It is not healed by time or distance. It is not healed by church attendance or Bible reading. It is not even healed by faith. It can be improved through counseling and learning better skills for how to process difficult emotions. We can even gain healing from this type of suffering through loving relationships with other people. In fact, this is usually a necessary step in the process. I am convinced, however, that within this category of suffering at the hands of other humans, there are depths of suffering so deeply embedded within our souls that the only way to reach a place of complete and total healing is through direct encounter with God Himself. This is not learning *about* Him. This is not even engaging in worship or prayer, though the value I have for those activities cannot be overstated. It is face-to-face with the One who formed you. It is the voice of your Maker spoken directly to you in such a way that you can mistake it for nothing and no one else. It is real, undeniable, and unable to be dismissed as imagination, hallucination, or imitation because of the direct and immediate effect it has on your soul.

And such radical encounter is absolutely necessary to heal certain levels of the pain of one human's violation of another because of the nature of this beast. I do not mean to imply that every instance of suffering at the hands of another human requires an intense encounter with the Lord in order to heal. No, I believe that God's intention is for us to eventually become so adept at the process of healing that we're able to do it rapidly and effectively, forgive easily, and return quickly to peace. Perhaps some reading this book will not have experienced the soul-crushingly deep wounds many others have—those who almost feel as though the pain of their existence is embedded into their identity—but some will. And this type of suffering has no natural tendency of its own to promote our growth or maturity, but rather to break, twist, and deform our souls. It is harmful, a violation of the design of humankind. It does not promote growth and often does not turn us to the Lord.

Many times, in fact, it drives us into all forms of addiction: alcohol, drugs, pornography, shopping, entertainment, eating, the admiration of people, falling in love, obsession, and all forms of brokenness and dissipation. Again, it is often suffering we are in no way responsible for, had no option to avoid, and no opportunity to escape. It breaks us. It misshapes our vision until we see everything through the lens of survival, hatred, bitterness, and pain. It causes us to become so obsessed with finding ways to meet the needs in us that were never met by others that we utterly ignore the one place where fullness can be found. It compels us to repeat patterns of abuse we ourselves suffered, either by continuously creating situations where we are victimized again and again or by becoming the perpetrators of abuse ourselves. It causes us to look inward to deposit self-pity, self-hatred, self-promotion, and all other words that begin with self except for self-reflection. It prevents us from looking inward and seeing the image of our Creator—the destiny placed within us. It prevents us from looking for any answers that don't immediately relieve our need for comfort, safety, admiration, or control.

This type of suffering is often found in broken and dysfunctional childhood families like my own. I did not choose to have my mother violently assault me. Being so young, I did not have the brain capacity to make any decisions. I did not choose to have the demonic oppression that gained access to me through the abuse, terror, and chaos of my childhood. I did not choose to have parents who ruined me, a sister who despised me, a body that rejected me, or a nervous system that destroyed me. I would even go so far as to say that, to a certain extent, I did not choose a number of situations in my life that occurred as a result of the brokenness I carried even in adulthood. Why? Because I didn't even have the capacity to choose something different, something other than what my brain and soul had been trained to do from birth. Could I have chosen healing? Sure, if I had known such a thing existed, and I did make that choice as soon as I had this realization. But until the healing had begun to take place, the desperateness of my own bondage had removed much of my choice.

We can know a tree by its fruit, and the natural state of the fruit of this kind of suffering is rotten. Without God's intervention, this type of suffering leads only to destruction and hopelessness. The world is filled with it. The people of the earth are buried beneath its staggering weight, desperate for answers, for hope.

As previously mentioned, I was raised with the poor theology that God *causes* our suffering to teach us lessons. So, I, at some point, had simply begun to believe that I was just born bad, a rotten apple in the barrel, someone who needed ample punishment to make up for my badness. I did not understand God wasn't the cause of my pain. My pain was caused by my parents exercising their free will in unrighteousness. It was caused by the demonic influences that had long ago attached themselves to my very wounded parents and continuously compelled and enticed them into evil. I did not understand that Jesus had already taken on the full punishment for sin so I wouldn't have to. I did not understand that by His stripes I was healed. Why would God go to all the trouble to heap the punishment for sin on the shoulders of His beloved Son if He then intended to simply go around punishing people anyway? It makes no sense. But I did not understand.

I did not understand that God's heart was broken for every moment of pain I experienced in my young life, and that He longed to heal my body, my soul, my heart, and my mind. I did not understand because I was so broken. I did not have the ability to understand.

CHAPTER 15

He heals the brokenhearted and binds up their wounds.
—Psalm 147:3

I began my journey of healing from this most difficult type of suffering at the age of thirty-four as my marriage was falling to pieces. I thought perhaps I would put in a good year of focused work on myself (since, toward the end of my marriage, I had made a number of decisions that were far from being in line with my beliefs and values) and be in fairly good condition for the rest of my life. Of course, anyone reading this who knows much at all about healing will laugh when they read that statement. William Paul Young, while speaking of his own twelve-year journey of healing, makes the statement that human beings were created in simply too complex a manner to go through healing quickly and easily. I have come to imagine it like a large ball of tangled necklace chains. Any woman who has ever had multiple necklaces with small metal chains become tangled together will know the excruciatingly slow process to which I am referring when it comes to untangling and setting them right. My oldest daughter has said to me that she believes it would feel like it was dishonoring the pain we experienced to just poof it all away in a moment. I tend to agree with her. And we also must remember that God does not just desire us to be free of pain. He desires us to be mature. And I can assure you that I have gained more maturity in the process of digging into the depths of my pain than from any other activity I've participated in. Facing, feeling, and no longer hiding from or coping with it, I invited God into the places of my deepest torment where I never could have climbed out myself.

You see, healing is painful. I have heard people say it does not *have to* be painful, but that's simply untrue in reference to the deep, ugly pain perpetrated by others against us. When we have pain of this kind within us, it is still there because we haven't allowed ourselves to fully experience it. And it will stay just where it is, causing us to live in dysfunction and brokenness until the day when we're finally willing to set aside our meager attempts at self-preservation and actually *feel* the full extent of it. Pain must be felt. So many people do not experience the healing they desperately need because they are afraid to feel the pain that has been buried deep under their countless coping mechanisms.

To some extent, I do not blame them. It is not for the faint of heart. There is some courage required. The collective hours, days, and years of my life that I have spent screaming out my soul to the Lord in pain as I sat there feeling the awful thing, letting it fill and wash over me until it had finally boiled over the top and left the pot have not been easy. They have been hard, but good—the hardest things I have ever done. But good. Because the pain left with those screams. Demonic spirits fled with those tears. The infection was purged. Holes were closed, and doors sealed.

Healing is painful. Not healing is painful. You can choose your pain and eventually move past it, or you can live for the remainder of your earthly life in the state of pain that someone else chose for you. One of them means acting as the powerful individual that God created you to be. The other means remaining forever a victim, allowing what was done to you once to be what remains done to you forever.

What I have discovered is that the only way out is through. The pain will never leave until you have allowed yourself to *go through it*. It will wrench your soul to pieces. But then it will be put back together, more beautiful than you have ever known it, more capable of love and true intimacy, more ready to carry the things God has placed in your heart.

And the sad truth is, the church has, for decades, centuries even, ignored this level of healing. They have glossed quickly over it, promoting the idea that all we need is salvation and an intellectual gospel and the work is finished. Even later, more Spirit-filled churches have come to the erroneous conclusion that all that's needed is to command healing to the soul, cast out the pain, declare it gone, as it were. As a result, the church has been run by broken orphans for centuries, harming as many people as they help, burning bridges, and smearing the name of

God by their actions. As Christine Cain has pointed out, no one goes to the altar, accepts salvation, and expects all of the cellulite and fat to immediately disappear from their body. They must set down the Krispy Kreme and get on a treadmill for that. We can no longer afford to teach or believe the lie that salvation immediately heals our souls either. It is an entirely separate process. It is the difference between the fact that we *are* saved (our spirits), we *will be* saved (our bodies), and we *are being* saved (our souls—in process). Each of these salvations is very specifically mentioned in Scripture. They are totally different and distinct experiences.

The time has come for a new type of leadership in the body of Christ. This leadership is fully healed, completely whole, not in the sense that they have arrived and will never need to heal or grow again, but in the sense that they've reached a place of maturity from which there is no turning back. In finding the place of healing and wholeness, there will be no regression. It is forward from here out. A leadership that lives authentically, openly, unafraid to admit when they are in need of more healing, more growth. Unwilling to judge those who are still in process, no matter what stage of the process they are in. Able to help people move forward in the process even as they themselves do. This leadership is not just filled with power, but also functions out of good character that remains on a path of continuous growth. Leadership in the church was never meant to be, "Look at me. I no longer make mistakes. You should admire me and listen to what I tell you." It was meant to be, "I've just found a new key and discovered the door it opens. I can't wait to show you."

CHAPTER 16

I have labored and toiled and have often gone without sleep;
I have known hunger and thirst and have often gone without
food; I have been cold and naked.

—2 Corinthians 11:27

In any discussion of suffering, there is always the question of why some individuals seem to suffer more than others. I will not pretend to believe there is a cut-and-dry answer that fits all situations. There are people who have suffered horrific violations, beyond what I can imagine, and there does not seem to be any purpose served by it other than for the enemy to ruin a human life. I don't believe this to be an accurate accounting, but it can certainly appear that way. But I do believe that *at times* there may be a reasonable explanation.

As I stated previously, God desires to use our experiences of suffering to further our own process of maturing and growth. I would, however, like to offer an alternate, perhaps more nuanced perspective in addition to the discussion of maturity.

You see, I believe that God often asks a greater level of suffering from those who are designed to carry a heavier burden. From Scripture and history, we can support this through the lives and deaths of the Apostle Paul, the other apostles, and Jesus Christ Himself. They each had some great work to accomplish. They each suffered greatly. One might come to the conclusion that deep suffering is even required in order to carry and accomplish some great works. There is something about the experience of suffering that better prepares us to bear certain burdens or complete certain missions.

Acts 9:15-16 states:

"But the Lord said to Ananias, 'Go! This man is my chosen instrument to proclaim my name to the Gentiles and their kings and to the people of Israel. I will

show him how much he must suffer for my name.'"

Immediately after Paul's encounter with Jesus on the road to Damascus, the Lord instructed Ananias that Paul must be told how much he would suffer for Christ. God did not feel it so necessary, apparently, to tell Paul all about the great ways he would impact the world for thousands of years beyond his own lifetime, the stadiums in which he would preach, or the books he would write (all of which he did do). But he did feel it was necessary to communicate to him that his mission involved suffering. Interestingly, we never see Paul having a crisis of faith over this knowledge. Within days of being told of his coming suffering, he begins to preach the Gospel (that he had just learned himself). When he is warned by both Agabus and by the Holy Spirit about what suffering and death await him if he travels to Jerusalem, there is no shrinking back, no second-guessing what he had heard God call him to do. It was part of his mission. He was unafraid of it, willing even to die, if necessary, to fulfill his assignment.

No one can deny that Paul suffered greatly. Paul himself summarizes his extensive suffering in 2 Corinthians 11. He does this absent any invitation to sympathy by the Corinthians, but instead, it appears, with a steadfast conviction that it was all done in the execution of his God-given mission. And no one can deny that in all of those instances, he was carrying out exactly what the Lord had called him to do. Claiming that God does not, in fact, *call* some people to a greater level of suffering is inaccurate and unbiblical. It seems clear to me that He does.

Paul could have said *no*. He could have refused the call, lived out his life in much more comfort than he ultimately did, and still have been granted entrance to heaven upon his death. There was nothing to compel him to follow the call of suffering but his deep and burning loyalty and love for the Lord his God. You can read throughout the New Testament, not only in the Corinthians passage, about the various difficulties Paul suffered in his life while on mission and his unwavering willingness to do so.

But wait, am I suggesting God orchestrated those instances of suffering in Paul's life as part of his mission? No, it is not that simple.

God, of course, knew those things would happen when he called Paul to go to each of the places he went and engage with the world in the way he did. But, no, I do not believe God inspired people to stone Paul, beat him, imprison him. But I do believe God asked him to take part in a *life of suffering*, to carry a weight that automatically brings with it a greater level of suffering. And he said *yes*. This yes led to persecution, physical harm, and, eventually, death for Paul. But it also led to an unprecedented spread of the Gospel throughout the known world within Paul's life, established much of the foundations of Christian belief, and illuminated the understanding of God for thousands of years beyond Paul's life. Many of us would love to have the kind of impact on the world that Paul had for the Kingdom. How many of us would as quickly sign up for the level of suffering he endured?

This is a hard concept to swallow, especially if your perspective is fixed on this lifetime. Why would some people be called to a life of suffering? As I stated before, Jesus suffered *unto something*. The burden He had to bear was the greatest ever borne. There is no weight any human has ever borne that compares. But some are asked to carry heavy burdens, nonetheless. Every person is called to accomplish supernatural and impossible things for the Kingdom of Heaven. Every person's mission is vitally important to the work of spreading heaven's dominion over the earth. Every person who is genuinely pursuing the Lord will, at some point, be asked if they are willing to experience pain, discomfort, or difficulty. But we can see from Scripture that there are people who are asked to carry a burden that is not glamorous. It is heavy. It does not center on fame, fortune, and fine dining, though I do not believe God is the least bit opposed to those things, especially when He has been given the opportunity to give them as gifts to His children. But the burdens of which I speak are done in the trenches. They are not carried out on stages, to applause. They are carried out in the darkest corners of the human soul. They are carried out in prisons and whore houses. They are carried out in the places where deep and unfathomable brokenness has long lay dormant, untouched by the light, in the mud, in the filth, in the squalor that is our inheritance from generations past. They are carried out holding abused and dying children in third-world orphanages, rescuing little ones from sexual slavery. They are carried out in the territories of drug cartels and corrupt world leaders. They are carried out where clean, proper people often fear to tread. They are not light. They are not easy, these burdens. They are heavy. They are hard. And there appears to exist a certain level of anointing reserved for those who accept such a call. Many a famous, impactful minister could tell of years spent in isolation, pain, and discouragement, battling demonic strongholds, human brokenness, and true depths of darkness before a single other human became aware of the call on their lives.

You see, the faith, hope, and perseverance that are grown in these trenches of suffering are often unable to be obtained through other means. The result of this is that the person who has endured the suffering and come out the other side often now carries the level of faith required to have a truly transformative effect on the world around them. This level of hope is necessary to stand unwaveringly in the midst of hopeless circumstances without faltering in the belief of God's impending arrival.

Imagine the maturity needed to carry the weight of such missions. This is the weight of His glory. These dark places are where His glory must go and where it can often be carried to the greatest effect. This is why God is looking everywhere for people who are unafraid to suffer. He needs glory carriers. And in our age of comfort and luxury, it's hard to find those who will volunteer for suffering. It is hard to find those willing to take things they have already suffered and, instead of using them as a perpetual means of garnishing sympathy, decide to use them to become mature enough to suffer even more, to carry even more glory, to have shoulders strong and broad enough to bear the weight of His coming Kingdom, His approaching glory. This is what we suffer unto, becoming capable of bearing the weight of God's glory to this world where suffering was always on the docket. We suffer unto holiness. Maturity that can carry the weight of glory is born in the fires of suffering. We are purged into holiness in the flames of suffering. I would not undo one moment of my life for any price, and I will tell you why.

CHAPTER 17

Then I heard the voice of the Lord saying,
"Whom shall I send? And who will go for us?"
And I said, "Here am I. Send me!"

—Isaiah 6:8

In my twenties, I had a dream. For years it plagued me, and I could not comprehend it, but I felt it deeply. It carried such weight of truth, even if my conscious mind didn't grasp what it was meant to communicate. I will recount it here, because it plays an important role in later revelations I received from the Lord about suffering.

In this dream, I was in some kind of basic training program for the military. Myself and many others were being housed in a large warehouse filled with makeshift beds and eating areas. We were all garbed in the type of military clothing worn commonly during basic training: matching green army fatigues, tank tops, and boots. On the wall was a bulletin board. Each day new papers would be posted to the board, and on each paper was the picture of one of the soldiers in training with a short description typed on the page next to it. I knew that these papers were the final assignments for each soldier in the training program. If the soldier passed the final assignment, then they would graduate, entering the full-fledged army.

The day arrived when my name and picture were posted on the board, so I followed our leader out the door of the warehouse toward my assignment. He led me to the top of a sheer cliff, extremely tall. At the bottom of this cliff was a beach, and beyond that, the ocean. Leading from the beach in a line out into the ocean were five enormous boulders. They were full of divots and jagged edges, not smooth or flat.

My leader lowered me down to the beach with these instructions. The sun was about to set. I would have until sunrise the following morning to walk out onto each of the boulders and collect a small coin that had been placed on each one. I must collect them all and return to the beach before sunrise to complete my mission.

This didn't seem so terribly difficult. It wouldn't be easy by any means. Despite their jagged and uneven surface, the rocks were likely to be slippery with spray from the sea, and it would be hard to keep my footing. But I believed I could do it. But then my leader gave me additional information about this mission.

He pointed to the beach, some distance from where the line of rocks began to jut into the ocean. I had not noticed until this moment a woman lying on the beach, apparently unconscious. She was blonde, pale-skinned, and gargantuan in size, wearing a garish pink dress. She was not necessarily a tall woman, but she was well beyond obesity in size. The girth of her was staggering, to say the least. My leader explained to me that the assignment of collecting the coins had belonged to her previously. It had been her graduation assignment. But when she had arrived on the beach, she had seen the difficulty of the assignment, lost hope of completing it, and sunk into unconsciousness on the sand. She had lain there ever since.

I could, my leader explained, complete my assignment, return to camp with all my coins, and meet the requirements for graduation. However, if I would carry this woman during the entire mission, it would be counted as her having also completed her assignment and she would be allowed to graduate as well. I looked at the woman, lying there, unconscious, and I accepted. I would carry her. I would complete my assignment and hers. I knew it would be difficult, but I had no desire to refuse. My leader made sure I understood that if I set her down at any time during my mission it would no longer count as her completion of the assignment. I must carry the full weight of her the entire time in order for her to graduate.

He left and I heaved a sigh, ready to begin. I removed every scrap of clothing I was wearing and stood completely naked in the darkening evening. I knew that my clothing would be a hindrance. It restricts movement and it was likely to get sprayed by the water and become unbearably heavy and even less flexible as a result.

I walked over to the woman and used what strength I had to hoist her up onto my shoulders, bending and staggering with the weight of her. It was completely dark by the time I reached the first rock. I cannot adequately explain the difficulty that I endured trying to find and pick up each coin while balancing this enormous woman on my back. The jagged rocks, the water, and the odd positioning of the coins and my own feet made it sometimes feel impossible. I found myself having to do bizarre feats of contortion at times, even once bending over completely backward in order to pick up a coin while still carrying the woman. Step after painful, shaking, sweating, exhausted step I worked my way out to the final rock and then back to the beach. It took the entire night. The sun was rising just as I reached the sand with two copper, two silver, and one gold coin in my hands.

I set the woman down on the beach and wrapped a white towel around myself. As I did, she revived. She looked around, seeming to realize that she had completed her mission. Without much care, she bounded toward the cliff where my leader and a small company of others had just arrived. They lowered the rope, and I tied it around her so they could pull her up.

They lowered the rope again, but I knew I did not need them to pull me up. Still wrapped in my towel, I climbed the rope to the top of the cliff. As I did, I couldn't help but notice the condition of my own musculature. My arms and legs were large, hard, and incredibly strong. The climb up felt like a stroll in the park, easy and effortless. I was shocked to realize this.

I arrived at the top to the congratulations of the small group of people waiting for me, including my leader. I had passed, he said. And so did the other woman. When I looked at her now, she had shrunk to the size of a small girl. She was still a bit chubby, but no longer obese. Her pink dress was much too big for her now, and she tripped over it as she began to run through the grass back toward the warehouse.

After I had been on an intense journey of healing for a few years, God brought this dream back to my mind over and over again. I knew it was important. I knew it was relevant. After some pursuit, I felt I finally had some understanding of at least some part of it. I believed that the assignment on the beach represented my mission in this life. And I came to an understanding that the very large woman I had chosen to carry represented the weight of generations before me in my mother's family line who were meant to have completed this assignment and did not.

One day as I was in prayer and worship in my room, God began to speak to me about this assignment. He brought to mind the horrible abuse of my grandmother, my mother, and myself. He revealed to me that the assignment I was to carry out was to break the generational curses of my mother's bloodline. The line of darkness ran thickly through that blood. I was to cleanse it.

Then, the Lord spoke nearly audibly and told me I was the Avenger of Blood for my family line. It was not a task. It was a title. It was a legal position. I knew that such a term existed in the Old Testament to refer to the closest relative of a murdered person whose job it was to avenge their death by killing their killer. I knew I was called to break generational curses, but now I realized it was a mission of vengeance—not against people, but against darkness, against evil. The Lord says vengeance is His, but I'm convinced this statement is in relation to human beings. In fact, the theologian George MacDonald claimed that even when God's vengeance is pointed toward people, it is aimed at the sin still resident within them. It is not for the purpose of their destruction; it's for their restoration. But the vengeance I was to take was not against any human being. It was against spiritual forces of evil in heavenly places. However, I knew my job was not to go searching for demonic spirits to torment in revenge. No, it was to scrape and burn and boil every last molecule of spiritual darkness from this bloodline until those spirits had no place to land, no hold to grip. I do believe the Bible when it says that one day we will judge angels (of the fallen variety I expect), and maybe at that time there will be some completion of this mission of vengeance. But for now, it was a mission of freedom, of driving out the giants, one by one, if necessary.

I wept for what felt like hours on my bed. Finally, I looked up at the

Lord and told Him, "I will do it."

The weight of that statement fell upon me like a mountain, like the entire ocean. It was a heavy thing I agreed to. It was not light. It was hard. It was His glory. And it was heavy. It required strong, mature shoulders.

"I will do it," I said again. And again. And again. "I will do it!" I screamed, tears pouring down my face and onto my shirt. "Here I am! Send me!"

And the strangest thing was, it felt somehow *retroactive*. Like I had already been doing this thing, and the moment of agreement to it had finally caught up with me. Of course, God is not bound by time as we are. It was all the same to Him.

But I did do it. I am still doing it—putting one foot in front of the other, refusing to go backward in this journey of healing and curse-breaking.

I struggled for a very long time with a spirit of victimhood. Please don't misunderstand. I *was* victimized, many times, by many people, in many ways. My life felt like one beating after another with no time to recover in between. But I had taken on a defeated mindset. "Why is it always me?" I felt powerless, to some extent, as though life just kept *happening* to me and there was nothing I could do. It was a mindset devoid of hope.

But I kept pursuing healing, deliverance, and forgiveness. When I lost everyone in my life, I sought out people I knew could help me. Though I rarely had much money, I spent it on SOZO and prophetic counseling. When I had no money, I simply made requests of people and apologized for being unable to pay them for their services. When there was no one and nothing, and even when there was, I spent hours upon hours, days, weeks, and months of my life, pursuing the presence of God, pursuing encounter, revelation, and healing. I listened to podcasts about psychological conditions and how to heal them. I read books, listened to sermons, and searched out every resource I could find on healing, deliverance, and forgiveness. At one time earlier on in my journey, I said a dangerous prayer. I told the Lord, "If You heal me, I will give You everything." And, like Hannah longing for a child and promising to give him to the Lord, I meant every word. I did not mean that I would withhold myself if He did not heal me. No. My desire was for Him to have every part of me regardless. Only, I knew that I wasn't capable of giving this gift to Him without my soul having been healed first. It would not work otherwise. Every now and then, I renew that vow.

If you truly desire healing, you can have it. I am living proof. But you must be relentless. I am still in the process of fully healing as I write this book, but I can tell you that I no longer recognize the person I was a few short years ago. I could not return to being her even if I desired to. And when you have moments, days, or even weeks when you feel like giving up, you must pull on the people you trust and the truths that you already know about God and what He has done in your life. Even if all your strength is gone, you must hang on to what you know. The collective hours of my life that I have spent unable to do any greater spiritual warfare or healing than lie on my couch with worship music playing, feeling as though I'd rather do anything than remain alive, but repeating to God, "I know that You are here even if I can't feel You. If You heal me, I will give You everything," are staggering. It is not easy, this healing. It is hard. But it is good.

CHAPTER 18

*You intended to harm me, but God intended it for
good to accomplish what is now being done,
the saving of many lives.*

—Genesis 50:20

One night during my healing process, after decades spent in a state entirely dissociated from my own emotions, I had finally been able to gain access to my feelings about what my mother had done to me as a child. They were the deepest, ugliest, most painful emotions I have ever experienced. There are no words. I lay in my bed in the dark, screaming into my pillows, my body curled up in a ball, every muscle contracting at the same time. This lasted for some time. In the middle of this, I saw the Father and the Holy Spirit come and sit beside me, cradling me in their arms, like a mother and father would do (I assumed). Never having experienced such a thing in my life, I had nothing with which to compare it. But really, there is no comparison.

I would like to clarify something before I continue. When I describe visions and encounters I've had with the Holy Spirit, I will invariably refer to her as "She." The more religious will, no doubt, find this unsettling. But I will state unequivocally that up to the writing of this book the Holy Spirit has only ever revealed Herself to me as a woman. Never once have I encountered the Holy Spirit as a man. If I ever do, I will be sure to refer to the Holy Spirit as "He" when discussing those encounters. While there does appear to be solid biblical translational ground upon which to stand in referencing the Holy Spirit absent male pronouns, at this point, I am neither claiming the Holy Spirit as definitively and only female nor as definitively and only male. I do not have the advantage of as in-depth a study and knowledge of the subject as I would like, nor have I received any new revelation on the topic beyond what's been discussed by better theologians than myself. It is also far afield from the purpose of this book. But like the blind man who said, "Whether he is a sinner or not, I don't know. One thing I do know. I was blind but now I see!" (John 9:25), all I can say is what experience I have had with the Living God. And so far, this has involved the Holy Spirit in a female form every time, and I will not dishonor the revelation God has given me by stubbornly referring to the Holy Spirit in a form in which She has not revealed Herself to me.

I am very conscious of the fact that spirit beings do not require and generally have no use for genitalia. However, reproductive organs are not the only differences between male and female beings, and I believe that for thousands of years now the church has massively and detrimentally downplayed the female attributes of God that are necessary for an effective and thriving body to exist. I will not make that same mistake simply to avoid offense. After all, every characteristic and attribute humanity has, including those traditionally considered more "female," are found in God, and we (male and female) are made in His image.

To return to my story, as I lay screaming, being cradled by the Holy Spirit and the Father, one thought kept coming to my mind. And so, I finally expressed it out loud.

"How could You?" I demanded of God. "How could You give me these people as my parents, knowing what they would do to me? How could You give me this assignment, knowing how it would destroy me?" I was angry, I felt betrayed by God. To be forced into such a life, such a mission. How could He make me do this?

"I didn't," the Father said simply, kindly.

"What do You mean, You didn't?" I asked Him, in some confusion.

"You chose this assignment," he replied, in a tone of voice that almost seemed to ask me why I didn't already know this information.

I was perplexed. But suddenly, the Lord spoke to me about my dream of the beach. I hadn't stopped to consider the warehouse where I was trained before being given my assignment. And suddenly I knew. The warehouse was heaven. It was in heaven before I was born on the earth. It was not, perhaps, the part of heaven where we look forward to living after this life, but it was heaven, nonetheless. In my dream, the warehouse had been a very secluded, separated space where only soldiers in training were housed and permitted. Suddenly, I understood that such a place exists in the realm of heaven—an area where those who have yet to come to earth are going through basic training for their entrance into the army of the Lord.

Amazingly, I saw, before my eyes, scene after scene of myself in heaven before being born on the earth. It was my spirit. There was no body or soul yet, just my spirit. I looked like a young adult or an older teen, but I was recognizable as myself. I had long, blonde hair and looked very athletic.

I saw a man standing in front of a group of people wearing army fatigues, holding up a piece of paper. He was explaining the assignment of breaking the curse in my mother's bloodline.

"Will anyone take this assignment?" he asked, looking around. I squared my shoulders and stepped forward.

"I will do it."

I saw myself in a massive library, sitting on the rung of a ladder, reading, reading, furiously reading. I knew what I was thinking. "I must know everything I can that could possibly help me accomplish my mission. I need to take every piece of knowledge I can with me."

I saw myself in a full suit of bright silver armor, training with a sword. "I must learn every skill I can to help me succeed in my mission."

"I chose this?" I asked the Father, astonished.

He didn't have to say yes. We both knew it. A great weight suddenly lifted from my shoulders. No longer was I a victim. I hadn't been forced into this life of suffering and misery at all. I had chosen it. I was powerful and free to choose. That didn't begin at my birth. It had started long before.

I had previously experienced my spirit leaving my body and participating in activities with the Lord while I slept. I nearly always immediately lost the memory of what we had been doing when my spirit reentered my body, but I retained the knowledge of having had the experience. Once, however, I began to wake and had the strangest sensation of being conscious in two places at once. My body and soul were comfortably lying in my bed while my spirit was somewhere in a forest with Jesus, who was teaching me many important things as if I were attending a school in the woods. When I began to wake, I was suddenly aware of how much knowledge my spirit had. My spirit felt ancient, as though it had been around a very long time and learned a great deal in that time.

I began to have the sense that my own spirit was rather annoyed with me. I (spirit) was deeply focused on something that Jesus and I were looking at together, a document of some kind, some sort of plan of action. I looked up suddenly and turned to Jesus, saying something to the effect of, "Oh no, she's waking up. I thought we'd have more time."

At the same moment, I (soul and body) had only a few moments of awareness of the things that so occupied the attention of Jesus and my spirit, and my very tiny physical brain was absolutely unraveled. It was genius. It was the definition of brilliance. It was all the answers we needed. It would change everything, the entire world. And then it was gone from my head like a puff of smoke, and my spirit was pulled back into my body. For the longest time, I could not shake the sensation that my own spirit found me tiresomely slow and stupid. And I found a new appreciation for the concept of the triune God. To have one part of yourself feel so irritated with the other parts of you really gives you perspective on how God can be three and one in the same instant. Not that God is ever irritated with Himself, but each part of the Trinity certainly seems to have their own unique contribution to the Godhead.

As I lay in the arms of the Father and the Holy Spirit (Jesus was also there, but not as central in the moment), all of these pieces, and many others that had previously puzzled me began to fall into place.

You see, I have always been a very studious and serious person. Don't misunderstand me, I enjoy humor. I have actually been known to be quite funny on occasion despite (or maybe because of) my autistic brain. I have also experienced the joy of the Lord until I began to build abdominal muscles from the laughter. But when it comes to the weightier matters of life, I am sober and solemn. If I have questions, I study a thing until I've read every notable opinion, tradition, and trail of evidence in existence about it. The greatest gift a person could give me is either a book or a gift card to a bookstore or to a website where I can buy books. I have hundreds of books and have given or thrown away many more than I currently own over the course of my life after reading them.

At the same time, I have always been physically driven and athletic. I don't feel I've even really exercised until my lungs have begun to burn and my face is as red as a cherry. I have always been determined to push both my mind and my body to their limits and then past them. Certainly, a part of this was from having been raised in such a performance-driven family. But much of it, I believe, was designed by God. And when I saw visions of my own spirit in heaven doing so much of the very things with which I have spent my life occupied, I suddenly understood myself.

Since becoming diagnosed with autism, I had begun to ask God, "Don't you think the things I suffered were quite enough without this difficulty?" Anyone who is close to an autistic person or is autistic themselves will understand to what I am referring. It is not an easy way to live within the current structure of society. People seem to love their fluorescent lights, their loud conversations, and their group projects. They love to bathe themselves in cologne and perfume, make sweaters that are scratchy, and just smile and laugh constantly. They love an inordinate amount of eye contact and having complex social interactions with real-life implications for anyone who does not perform them correctly. Every conversation is like an exam. Especially in a world where social rejection is layered on top of the already existent difficulties of autism, it simply seemed unnecessary to me. "Wasn't my suffering enough?" I had asked Him at several points in time.

But now I understood. You see, my brain, which could hyperfocus on accomplishing a task and nothing else until that task was completed, which had a bizarrely efficient pattern-recognition mechanism, matched perfectly my spirit, who had determined long before my birth to do nothing but complete the mission until it was done and find every answer necessary to do so.

I had a new understanding of what I had begun to consider "wasted years" of my life. There were a good fourteen years between my salvation experience and when I finally began to know who God truly was and then began to heal. These were the years in which I made most of the life decisions that I would later come to regret for the harmful effects they had on myself and others. *Wasted years*, I thought. But looking back at my educational choices, the things I spent my free time studying, the rabbit holes I would travel down on YouTube for days at a time, I began to realize something significant. My own spirit was pushing, prodding me for that entire time, in fact, for my entire life. "Figure it out. Find the answers. Break the curse." I had felt driven to understand the complex workings of the human soul for thirty-four years before I even really began to do so. But that entire time, my spirit was on mission. Just because I didn't realize it consciously didn't mean that I hadn't been reaching for the goal, pushing toward it my entire life. I thought they had been years that the locusts had eaten. He restored them to me in a moment. And I realized that without my autistic brain, I would not have been able to bear that constant driving force. I would have been utterly worn out by the constant push to find the answers. I would not have matched myself. Not for a moment do I believe that the God who designed every part of me would have made each of them in conflict with the others. The enemy causes us to be against ourselves, not the Lord.

Now, please understand, I am not making a claim that there's no case for the healing of autism. Updated scientific research has shown that certain expressions of autism do not really fall into the category of a "disability" the way it has traditionally been understood. It certainly makes life difficult, but only because the structures of society are not conducive to autistic people living and functioning in the way that their brains naturally operate. The expectations of the greater social machine tend to punish autistic people for living as their authentic, genuine selves.

But autism, in many ways, is really just a different way of the human brain functioning, a way that prioritizes different aspects of life than the neurotypical brain. The autistic brain is not necessarily a brain in dysfunction by default. It is often simply a brain with an alternative system of functioning that can seem incompatible with other systems (though I don't believe this to be inherently true). Autistic brains have a different operating system than non-autistic brains, similar to computer systems like Microsoft and Apple, which both function and accomplish necessary tasks but seem to be incompatible with each other.

I do believe that the church has some length to go in its approach to individuals with autism and other neurodivergent brains, but as with any topic, there is rarely a cut-and-dry answer that fits every person. There is a great deal of nuance to examine. Some autistic individuals suffer so greatly that they're unable to really function in relationships with other people in a meaningful and productive way. For some, it prevents them from communicating at all. For some, the overstimulation of the world around them is so all-encompassing that it significantly diminishes their ability to participate in needed life activities and skills. In my belief, there is absolutely a place for the healing of autism when the autistic person is experiencing dysfunction that prevents them from participating in normal life activities every human should be able to do (physical self-care, communication, learning, etc.). Though it does appear that such extreme difficulties can also be, at times, the result of co-occurring conditions rather than directly the result of autism alone. However, I don't believe that the "healing" of autism is necessary for many autistic people because their difficulties are not the result of any inherent inability to function; they're simply the result of their operating system clashing with the world's expectations.

I certainly wouldn't mind some aspects of my own autism being changed. For example, there are certain types of information that my brain cannot remember without specific prompts. No matter how many times I repeat the same scenario, my brain will not keep track of the information unless it is framed in a very specific way. This has caused me to inadvertently hurt people who I love because they have felt that I don't take them and what I know about them into consideration when making decisions.

However, while there are certain types of information for which my brain is incapable of connecting the dots, there are other types of information with which my brain makes connections and sees patterns so easily that I sometimes struggle to find other people with whom I can discuss these topics. This has caused me a great deal of difficulty in many ways, certainly. People have often told me that they have the impression that I'm prideful or think that I'm always right. I have also been told that I don't care about people very much, which could not be further from the truth. It's often difficult for me to do things like sit quietly in a meeting where a dozen other people slowly crawl toward a solution to a problem that I had solved in my mind about a minute into the discussion. Sometimes they do not land on the solution at all, and I am torn between stating what appears to me an obvious answer to their obstacle and having people dislike me and keeping silent and watching a project fall to pieces.

This, however, is not some inherent inability to function; this is a difficulty with a very efficiently functioning portion of my brain not meeting the social expectations of others. And this aspect of my brain has produced an immense amount of good in my life as well— understanding the ways of God, understanding Scripture through lenses that were never taught to me, and even strategizing for how to win a soccer game. And I've realized that these parts of my brain have been indispensable in the greater strategy of my life mission. In His goodness, God knew how desperately I wanted to do well and complete my mission. He gave me the tools I would need to do so, my brain being one of those.

As these things began to fall into place in my mind, I let out deep, shuddering sobs. "I did it," I said over and over again. "I did it." I had finally figured out the greatest mystery of my life, who I was, and why I was on my very specific and difficult path.

"You did so well," they said to me. "We're so proud of you." The words were so pregnant with love that it's difficult to describe with nothing but words on a page.

I wept for the sheer relief of it. I wept because I could finally understand. I wept because I suddenly knew how foolish I had been to volunteer for this assignment. Like Adam and Even in the garden. God had told them that disobedience would lead to death, but they didn't know what death *felt like*. Not until it was a part of their reality.

"That was a really stupid decision," I said to the Father through choking sobs. He laughed, and I wept all the more from relief. "I want to go home," I cried, shoulders heaving with sobs. "I want to go home. I want to go home." I meant heaven. I could feel it. I was hovering on the edge of it as we talked, and my spirit longed for nothing else.

"You can come home any time you want," Holy Spirit said to me gently. I felt like a college student, like my mother was telling me to come back on the weekends so she could wash my laundry.

"I want to come now," I said. "But only for a little while," I added, recalling that I still had children to raise.

Instantly my body began to lose consciousness, and I could feel my spirit pulling up and away from it. I began to lift up into the air, but I suddenly became afraid that I wouldn't return, and my children still needed me. But I touched heaven first. I said it again, and the same thing happened. And I touched heaven again. Multiple times I began to leave my body and was then pulled back by my own fear. But I momentarily basked in the substance of heaven first.

At a previous time, I had had to have general anesthesia for a surgery to repair my broken foot. I awoke as my spirit was returning to my body, knowing without a doubt that I had just spent a lengthy time with the Father having some adventure. I wanted to ask them to put me back under again because I wasn't ready to be conscious. It was the best I had ever felt in my life. My semi-conscious brain even began to try to think of ways that I could convince them that I needed another general anesthesia.

But this was more. I touched heaven itself with full awareness. And unlike here, heaven is *alive*. It is made of joy, I think, or love. Honestly, they might be the same thing. At least, I could not tell the difference there.

For the next two days after this, I did little more than stare at a wall and repeat the phrase to myself over and over, "I want to go home." My children, who are quite used to me doing strange things, even began to wonder if I was alright. I was so distracted. I will tell you that I knew my children needed me to finish raising them. But if they had not, I would have happily stayed in heaven forever. During those next two days, I even began telling God that as soon as my kids were adults, I was ready to go. The goals and dreams I had for the remainder of my life, the future plans, the ministries, and the signs and wonders I intended to take part in seemed trivial. "Someone else can do those things," I thought. "They don't need me."

When I've heard believers state that "This world is not our home," I knew it was theologically correct in the sense that we were designed to live in a state of perfection where spirit, soul, and body are all whole and simultaneously alive and aware. This isn't possible in the current state of the earth. We are meant to live in a state of eternity. But I never knew what home actually meant until that encounter. The day when all things are made new and we are finally able to live on earth and in heaven simultaneously is a day that burns in my heart constantly.

I know many believers who fear the return of Jesus to the earth. Life will be cut short. Suffering may take place. What if I never get married, graduate college, have my career? I say, "Come, Lord Jesus." I can hardly bear the wait. Those other things, those other pursuits are nothing in comparison.

I will tell you that when I die, if someone raises me from the dead without an exceptionally compelling reason (and likely even if they have an exceptionally compelling reason), they ought to be prepared for me to be furious with them. This encounter gave me a great deal to think about in regard to raising the dead, especially dead believers. It seems like a downright unkind thing to do to someone who's already in heaven.

I also came away from this encounter liking and respecting myself in new ways and far more than I had ever done in my entire life. "I'm pretty cool," I kept telling God, repeatedly shocked by the revelation. Until that moment, I had never known what it was to like myself. Even when I had learned to stop hating myself, I couldn't honestly say I had begun to actually like myself. And I suddenly did. All at once I realized that God's creation of me was nothing less than brilliant. Verses such as, "I am fearfully and wonderfully made" (Psalm 139:14) started making sense. Many things made sense, including the suffering I had experienced.

One of the best things that I took away from this encounter was the deeply embedded feeling that my Father trusted me to do hard things. If He hadn't, I suspect He would have suggested an alternate assignment to me when I volunteered for this one. But He trusted that I could endure the suffering and be victorious. He trusted that I have what it takes to be a carrier of His glory to the earth.

My life has not been easy in many respects. But it has been good. It has been horrifically painful. But it has been good.

As I sit here writing this, I am fully aware of areas in which more healing is needed and more deliverance. I am also cognizant of the fact that there are still areas in me that need healing of which I am not yet aware and probably won't become so until a situation in my life triggers some unexpected reaction. But I'm committed to the healing. I am committed to growth. And most significantly, I am committed to going wherever He directs me and addressing whatever He shows me. I choose to have no places where He is not allowed. I choose to have no points at which I will say, "Here, God, and no further."

I have heard that sin and darkness cannot survive in His presence, that they are burned up. For some people I've known, this has caused them to fear getting too close to Him. The burning will be painful, they're afraid. I find myself often thinking, "Burn me up, Lord." If that's what is necessary, then burn me up. Even if I die, what a way to die! There are things and there are people, the loss of whom would be devastatingly painful. But there is only One without whom I simply cannot live. And I have told Him that if He will heal me, He can have everything. And I'm determined that everything He shall have.

CHAPTER 19

For God will bring every deed into judgment,
including every hidden thing,
whether it is good or evil.

—Ecclesiastes 12:14

I'd now like to bring up a topic related to suffering that can be, to some, a shocking concept to examine. A book on suffering simply would not be complete if there was no analysis of the biblical book of Job. This book, which many people have found to be confusing, a confirmation that God initiates suffering to His faithful followers in order to teach them lessons, or simply a book to be avoided, creates a great deal of theological difficulty across the spectrum of Christian perspectives.

I myself have not traditionally enjoyed reading Job. One might think with a background like mine, I could relate to a man in a place of deep suffering, but in all transparency, I have found little comfort and fewer answers in its pages. The lengthy monologues of his "friends" sound precisely like the last thing on earth I would wish to hear in a time of difficulty, and I frankly believe the best action they took in the story was to sit down and be silent for a week. I'm sure Job would have preferred they remain that way. His wife was little better at comforting him in his misery.

Sitting by and passively watching as some evil being harms one of His children seemed an awful lot like something my own father would have done (did), and the apparent comparisons with God in this book made it, for most of my life, nearly unbearable to read.

One reason why I, and I believe many others, have found Job difficult to read (aside from the numerous grating speeches of his so-called friends) is the sense of utter injustice that seems to pervade the story. It appears at first glance as though God is perfectly happy to allow an evil being to dictate the circumstances of Job's life for no other reason than to prove a point. An altogether human response to the assertions of the accuser in this story, it appears to serve no other purpose than to satisfy God's pride. This picture of God seems to little resemble the God I see displayed throughout the remainder of Scripture, and I've often wondered why on earth the book of Job was even allowed in the Bible, given its confusing and seemingly contradictory presentation of God's nature. I have long felt that this interpretation simply cannot be true and that we are dramatically missing the mark if we simply settle for understanding this story as God having the capricious and impulsive nature of a man, as this book seems to imply.

In our attempt to understand this story, I'd first like to point out several interesting points about Job's ordeal that must be acknowledged. One of these is how he does not waver in his belief that he is undeserving of his afflictions. It is clear that he does not believe his suffering is the result of his own sinful ways. His friends are convinced that God is punishing him for some action he took that he either does not remember or that he is hiding from them. They attempt to convince him to buy into punishment theology, but he is, thankfully, having none of it. He asserts that his troubles are from God (a mistaken perception), but remains convinced of his own innocence, refusing to accept the punishment-based claims of his friends. It's clear at the end of the book that Job is vindicated; his troubles are not a punishment from God and his friends are wrong.

But many people's questions about the book revolve around the dynamics of God's conversation with another being called the accuser or adversary. Many English translations of the Bible translate this word accuser/adversary as the proper name "Satan," indicating that it is, in fact, the leader of the heavenly rebellion. He who was cast to the earth for his pride appears to be engaging in casual conversation with the Lord. To be sure, Satan is called the accuser of the saints (Revelation 12:10) and our adversary in many places in the Bible, but I don't necessarily believe it means every being in an accusatorial position is, in fact, Satan. It could be Satan, but there does not seem to be a direct connection made to the being we call the devil and the accuser who's standing before God in this story. There is another possibility I'd like to discuss in the following paragraphs, but whomever this accuser is, he seems to bait God into allowing the tormenting of Job. Many people find this to be a strange concept. Is God so unstable as to be swayed into allowing His children to be harmed by powers of darkness to prove a point, to satisfy pride?

What may be even stranger is the fact that God Himself is the one who initially brings Job to the attention of this accuser. "Have you considered my servant Job? There is no one on earth like him; he is blameless and upright, a man who fears God and shuns evil," God asks (Job 1:8). Why is He pointing Job out to a being that's clearly an enemy of the man and has his harm in mind? This being is already accusing Job's character before it has even had the opportunity to be tested. This being is no friend to Job. Why would God place Job in this position?

There does seem to be a deeper dynamic taking place here than it would at first appear, deeper than we have traditionally understood throughout church history. Why would God allow what appears to be a power of darkness, possibly the devil, to torment one of His beloved children? Why would a good Father stand by and not only allow, but condone, the harm of His faithful son? This does not line up with the picture of a loving Father we see represented elsewhere in Scripture.

There is an important spiritual truth, an underpinning principle at play in the life of Job, however, that we must bear in mind while reading his story. I made brief mention of this truth earlier in this book, but it is now necessary to revisit the concept in greater depth.

The spiritual world has laws. God is the King, and one day every knee will bow and every tongue confess His lordship. So, He is the maker of laws in the spiritual world, just as higher ruling bodies make laws in most countries across the world. However, it's important to note that Supreme Court Justices, policemen, senators, and even the President of the United States are all subject to the laws of the land in which they live, even if they are the ones who wrote those laws and enforce them. But make no mistake, God is also Judge, the highest of all judges, in fact, and in this role, He upholds the laws that He created to govern the spiritual realm.

At the end of this age when Satan and his demons are locked away forever in the lake of fire, all things will be made new, and evil will no longer have access to creation. It is also clear, however, that until that most desirous day should arrive, the powers of evil have a legal right to exercise their will to a certain extent among humanity in an attempt to achieve their own ends.

We can see an example of this in the story of the demoniac in Matthew 8. When the man is delivered by Jesus from a legion of demons, the demons speak directly to Jesus: "Have you come to torment us before the time?" They then ask of Him to be sent into a herd of pigs, and, shockingly, He obliges and sends them into the pigs (who subsequently propel themselves over a cliff).

Why did the demons say, "before the time," and why did Jesus acknowledge their request, allowing them to go into the pigs? It is clear to me that Jesus has no compassion for tormenting demonic spirits. This is plain from His many works of deliverance. The most reasonable conclusion to me based on His brief conversation with these spirits is that they had a legal right to be here on this earth. They seem very much aware that there is a time coming when they will be tormented, when their time here in the realm of the earth will be over. But clearly their time has not yet come, meaning they have been allowed to carry out their harassing and tormenting on the earth based on some legal permission. Jesus does not allow them to remain in the man to whom He is ministering, again, because God does not initiate, allow, or approve of the suffering that takes place in His people. He healed and delivered every person who asked it of Him, without exception, just as He desires to do with us. But the fact that demonic spirits are on the earth and carrying out their torment on human beings appears to be permitted based on a legal right.

In Job's situation, the principle at play is also one of legal proceeding. The Bible holds a surprising number of legal references when detailing God's works in the realm of the spiritual. Psalm 82 tells us that "God has taken his place in the divine council; in the midst of the gods he holds judgment." Though this verse seems to be, perhaps, the most direct reference to a heavenly council, anyone who has any familiarity with courtrooms or matters of a legal nature will find numerous others throughout Scripture.

At the very beginning of the book of Job, we are told that a group of angels came to "present themselves before God" and that the accuser also came with them (Job 1: 6). What does it mean that they came to present themselves before Him? And why would an accuser (possibly the devil) be coming into the presence of God? If it was Satan, was he not thrown out of heaven and God's presence? And here they are having a chat—a seemingly random, almost congenial conversation.

If we view God through the lens of Father, provider, or any of his familial roles, this story is appalling. It is unjust, unfair, and out of character for God. What becomes clear, however, when we wear the lens of God as Judge rather than God in one of His various other roles is that there is a legal proceeding taking place in these verses. The angels presented themselves before God because they are members of the divine council, the divine governmental body, and the court of law was now in session. Dr. Michael Heiser wrote an excellent book to discuss the topic of the divine council called *The Unseen Realm*. For an in-depth look at this topic, I would highly suggest it as an informative resource.

Once we see that the court of heaven is in session at the start of the story of Job, we can easily recognize the presence of the accuser as nothing more noteworthy than a prosecuting attorney attending a day in court. This being is clearly in the camp of darkness—accusation against God's people comes from that realm—but he clearly also has a legal standing to occupy that position, and God, the Judge, is legally obligated by His own laws to hear the prosecution.

God created the spiritual laws that govern the heavens, and you can be certain that any law created by God is good. And in His own goodness, holiness, and perfection, He will not violate His good laws, even if fallen creatures use these laws at times to attempt to produce evil. If, as seems likely, this spiritual legal system was created before the fall of mankind, and even before the fall of Satan and his angelic followers from heaven, we can be certain that the intention of this system was not for the harm of God's people or to provide space for beings of darkness to indict or torment us. Rather, this system is for proper governance of creation. The fact that fallen spiritual beings attempt to use this legal system to their advantage against God's people does not negate the goodness of the system or of its Creator.

An excellent resource on the topic of this spiritual legal system and its operations is a group of books written by Robert Henderson specifically about the courts of heaven. For a much more extensive look at understanding this topic, I would highly suggest reading any of his books on the subject.

But now we must try to answer the question of why God pointed out Job specifically to this accuser. I think we can safely surmise that the accuser in this scenario, whether Satan or some other being of darkness, was in the courtroom of heaven specifically to accuse those faithful to God. That is an accuser/prosecutor's job, after all. He brings charges against those he believes have violated the law, and we know the camp of the enemy is always on the lookout for reasons to accuse the saints. This first chapter of Job also states that the accuser had been roaming around the earth prior to arriving before God. It seems quite likely that this roaming involved a great deal of the collection of information (evidence). I suspect the accuser was building multiple cases against numerous individuals to present before the Judge in court. In case there is any question, we have all violated the laws of God, and there is an accuser always wanting to bring this before the Judge and have us pronounced with a legally damning sentence. Thankfully, we have an advocate (lawyer) in Jesus Christ (1 John 2:1) who stands in the legal gap on our behalf. In this specific circumstance, however, it seems likely that the courts of heaven were in session for much more than the examination of Job's life. If a human judge oversees dozens of cases per day, I think we can be confident that there are always many cases on the legal docket of heaven's courtroom.

It seems likely to me that the prosecutor was presenting a stack of cases during this session of court and that Job's would have been presented eventually, regardless of whether or not God had brought him to direct attention. I have no inside information on this specific instance, but it seems quite likely to me that God pointed out Job's case because it was a fairly open-and-shut one. Likely it was the last case that the accuser wanted to present, knowing how little evidence he had with which to make his case. Job was righteous. Even the accuser could come up with no dispute of Job's character beyond what he thought Job *would do* if his blessings and protection were removed. There was no current wrongdoing with which to accuse him. It was almost as if God were saying to the accuser, "If you want to make accusations, good luck trying it with Job." It was almost as if God were so confident in Job's faithfulness and righteousness that He was taunting the accuser with the fact that he would most certainly fail in any attempt to prosecute Job for a crime.

And based on the response, the accuser knew this as well. "Well, yes," he seems to admit begrudgingly, "of course there's nothing of which to accuse him. You've given him everything. He has no reason to complain" (this is, obviously, a paraphrase). The accuser seems almost to sulkily object to Job's good fortune, as if it were unfair to him personally, which seems to indicate that he, at least, believed himself to have some preexisting right to accuse God's people and had been denied that right because of Job's righteousness (which he views as being the result of Job's many blessings). If God was prompting the accuser to focus his attention on Job when attention would otherwise not have landed there, we can be sure that God was not constructing a scenario for Job to suffer harm. It seems much more likely, and appears supported by the accuser's own response, that the accuser would rather not have examined the case of Job because of the lack of evidence. But God was not allowing him off the hook so easily. Job's life would be examined, and there would be found no evidence with which to indict him.

I believe that reading the story of Job through a legal lens rather than a familial lens is absolutely essential to understanding its truths and purpose. It seems to me that so far, we are on good footing with Job's story when we view it through this lens. But what comes next is often the most difficult portion of the tale. The accuser requests to have Job's blessings and protections removed from him, not for anything he has done, but as a test of his character. Minus the blessings and protections, would Job be an unrighteous man after all?

This exchange can trigger feelings of injustice if we forget to understand it through the lens of legality. The accuser and the Judge are still in a courtroom at this point in the narrative, and their discussion is still of a legal nature, not a conversational one. If we keep this in mind, then one thing becomes clear: if God grants this accuser the ability to bring this test of character to Job, there must be a legal standing upon which the request was made. God judged it within the legal right of the court prosecutor to prove or disprove Job's faithfulness, righteousness, and loyalty to God—a right that had seemingly been denied because of Job's lack of notable sin.

I cannot state this unequivocally, but perhaps this theory is valid: in such a circumstance as a blameless, upright servant of God, the legal right to attempt to find fault with people allows such a being as the accuser to try to tempt them into sin or unfaithfulness in order to be able to make a final statement about that person's righteous character before the court of heaven.

Job's story is not the only circumstance that appears to support this theory. Another example of it can be found in Luke 22:31–32. Here, Jesus tells Peter that Satan has asked to "sift you like wheat." Jesus then tells him, "I have prayed for you so that your faith may not fail. And when you have returned, strengthen your brothers." It is quite clear from this passage that Satan has made a request to "sift" Peter, and the request has been granted. If it had not been, why would Jesus have needed to pray for Peter's faith not to fail?

This brings me to yet another type of suffering we need to understand. It is an example of a narrow circumstance in which God does not initiate, or even necessarily allow, suffering, but a legal statute seems to be at play that permits a period of trial to take place in a person's life. This "sifting" appears to be the case with both Job and Peter. God appears to consent to this based on a spiritual legality. However, for someone who is truly loyal to Yahweh, it appears that this sifting does not ultimately turn out to be a destructive event long term.

From my understanding of Scripture, both Job and Peter were great lovers of the Lord. They were committed, devoted, and determined to follow Him. Job even often made sacrifices on behalf of his children in case of unintentional sins, and Peter had only just made dramatic proclamations about his undying devotion to Jesus and his intent to never abandon Him. I do not see examples of such testing in Scripture of individuals who had not so completely devoted themselves to following the Lord (perhaps because they no longer have anything notable with which to be currently accused in the courtroom of heaven). And so, I would argue that such sifting is reserved for those who've already grown to a certain level of spiritual stature and maturity. In fact, it appears to be largely a test to see just how deeply their professed loyalty to their God runs. Job's temptation was to curse God and accuse Him of wrongdoing. Peter's was to deny and abandon Christ in His hour of need in order to save his own skin. Each of these was a test of loyalty and faithfulness.

Now, obviously, God already knows how deeply such loyalty runs in a human heart. But the devil does not, and the human does not. It appears to me that our accuser has a legal right to determine the true status of our loyalty and faithfulness to God, and I strongly suspect that after such a time of testing is completed (because it's clearly a limited period of time reserved specifically for sifting), the person who has come through the testing is now prepared to carry a much greater weight of the glory of God to the earth. They now know deeply within their own hearts the state of their own devotion to the Lord.

It is reminiscent of the process of tempering glass. Glass is tempered by being exposed to extreme heat for a period of time and quickly cooled. After this process is complete, the glass is five times stronger than it was in its original state. It can carry a great deal more weight without cracking than it previously could. I believe we could just as easily call sifting "tempering."

I don't believe the process of sifting will necessarily apply to the average, run-of-the-mill Christian in the modern West because it appears that many of today's comfortable Christians have not pursued God's lordship in their lives to the extent where sifting would be legally warranted. However, we should all hope to reach such a place within our lifetimes.

In the case of Job, he did not curse God or accuse Him of wrongdoing, despite his many trials. However, he wished for death. He cursed the day of his birth. And he was angry with God, nonetheless. Peter abandoned and denied Christ and suffered a great deal in his soul over his own actions. But is sifting meant to be something that we are able to "get through" on our own? I believe sifting is, in fact, meant to be so difficult that if it wasn't for what we already knew about God, we would absolutely fail without question. It's meant to bring us face-to-face with the limits of our own capacity to trust the Lord. You see, I believe the real test is *faith*.

If faith is the certainty of what we hope for and the assurance of what we do not see, then Job's faith in God was greatly tested. He no longer saw any evidence of God's goodness, blessings, or favor in his life. But because of his history with the Lord, he held stalwartly onto what he did know: God is good, He does not do wrong, and this suffering is not a punishment from God for some wrongdoing. Even when he could make no sense of his suffering, Job held to those simple truths. Job is addressed on his poor attitude, and certainly, his anger toward God. But he is also commended because, in the depths of his sorrow, he held onto what he knew. He kept his faith.

It was Peter's faith that was sifted, just like Job's, his faith that Jesus would not abandon *him*. Peter's betrayal of the Lord was based on a desire to save himself from the difficulty that would have accompanied remaining with Jesus and openly acknowledging Him as they dragged Him before His accusers. You see, self-preservation is always rooted in a lack of trust that God will continue to be with and care for us in the midst of difficulty or danger. So, Peter's lack of faithfulness to the Lord at that moment was really a lack of faith that God would remain with him through the difficulty. He fell into what was likely a long-standing pattern of looking out for himself because he didn't expect anyone else would. I have some experience in this area and recognize it in Peter's knee-jerk reaction to Jesus' predicament. After his fight response had passed, his flight response took over and he left behind the One he had only just sworn to never abandon. Peter did not fare, perhaps, quite so well as Job under the circumstances. But Jesus already knew this would be the case, otherwise, why would He have said, "when you return," clearly implying a failure from which Peter would need to return? You see, the fact that Jesus is our Mediator allows us access to the grace that lets us return to Him when we have utterly failed.

Jesus also tells him to strengthen his brothers upon his return. It appears to me that after having gone through this painful sifting, Peter suddenly has the capacity to give away strength to others who may need it. The sifting is not intended to make Peter weak, nor for God to see where Peter's heart really is (He already knows). It seems that one purpose of the sifting, or at the very least, a significant byproduct of it, is that Peter is now stronger than he previously was. He now has something to offer those who may need strengthening.

I find Job's statement in chapter 9:33–34 fascinating: "If only there were someone to mediate between us," speaking of God and himself, a distinctly legal notion. We know that Jesus is named the Mediator between God and men (1 Timothy 2:5–6). When Jesus tells Peter that Satan has asked to sift him, he says, "I have prayed for you so that your faith may not fail." Peter seems to have the Mediator Job longed for: Jesus in the flesh. In Job's time, Jesus had not yet been incarnated on the earth, yet he knew a mediator was needed. He seemed quite aware that what was required in his situation was a good lawyer. For the post-resurrection believer, we have a permanent Mediator, a lawyer in the courtroom of heaven, in the form of the resurrected Jesus Christ. He Himself has already paid the price for our lawbreaking.

When the accuser attempts to make a case against us now in the courts of heaven, the blood of Christ speaks a better word (Hebrews

12:24). We do not need to rely on our own righteousness, because we have been made the righteousness of God in Christ (2 Corinthians 5:21). No matter how often or with how much evidence the accuser presents his case against us, we are declared innocent, righteous, in good standing with the law and with God Himself. When the Judge examines our case, He does not see our sin or failure; He sees the perfection of Christ, the innocence and purity of His own Son. As a Father, of course He recognizes the areas where we continue to need growth and healing in our characters and souls and is committed to this growth in us even more than we are. But as the Judge, He sees only a righteous, unindictable person, every imperfection utterly erased by the blood of Christ. We have no need to hold tightly to the belief in our own righteousness before God as Job did. When accusations come against us, we need only to recall the righteousness of Jesus Christ and know that every accusation against us has fallen flat before God, our Judge. If the prosecutor in heaven's court was hesitant to try the case of Job before the Judge because of lack of evidence, imagine just how frustrated are the plans of the accuser who goes to present our case before God on this side of the cross. All the work of gathering evidence against us utterly wasted when positioned against the blood of Christ.

The only question that remains for me regarding this unique brand of suffering—sifting—is whether or not it is something that believers still may potentially face today. Admittedly, both prominent examples of such sifting in Scripture occurred prior to the death and resurrection of Christ. There is validity to the question of whether or not it was a distinctly pre-resurrection phenomenon. I tend to fall on the side of the belief that we do still see examples of sifting in believers in our day. Sifting, at its core, is really a time of testing for an individual that firmly establishes the extent of their loyalty to the Lord. It truly tests both their faith and their character to an extent well above the average experience of trial and suffering, and even above what we commonly think of as "wilderness seasons" in our lives as believers, but with a very specific result in mind. I have heard many individuals who are doing powerful works for the Kingdom of Heaven talk about seasons of intense trial in their lives where their faith was pushed to its absolute limits and there was nothing onto which they could tightly hold besides the certainty of the goodness and faithfulness of God against all apparent evidence. They may not have called it sifting, but both the process and the result appear to follow this pattern.

God does not initiate suffering against His children, but He is infinitely able to use the plans and schemes of the enemy (even those based on legal right) to our benefit and growth. At the end of the book of Job, God blesses the later era of Job's life significantly more than even the blessings he had prior to his suffering (Job 42:12). Peter, after his difficult ordeal, returns with enough strength to give away to his brothers and goes on to be one of the most prominent and powerful figures in the spread of the Gospel throughout the earth. It is clear to me that for those whose hearts truly are for God, regardless of how imperfectly it is done, the sifting results in not only personal benefits to the one being sifted in the form of dramatically increased growth and maturity (and, in Job's case, material blessings), but also blessings for those with whom they come into contact.

From my own seasons of intense suffering, I know there is nothing that has drawn me so close. Nothing else has so firmly established my belief in the goodness of God and His absolute faithfulness than to praise Him in the midst of the pain, to flatly refuse the lies offered by circumstantial evidence against God's character, but instead, like Job, to fall down and worship as my life has fallen apart around me, to declare to the atmosphere that my circumstances do not define His place or His character. Because of what I have gained from doing so, I would not undo these times of trial for any prize or benefit that man could offer. Suffering has taught me more about the goodness of God than any other experience. I refuse to trade this knowledge for anything.

CHAPTER 20

Who is this coming up from the wilderness
leaning on her beloved?

—Song of Solomon 8:5

Bearing some close similarities to the concept of sifting is yet another form of suffering that nearly all true believers will face at one time or another in their lives. This is the wilderness.

Many books have been written, many sermons given, and much analysis discussed about the concept of the wilderness, I believe, because it is such a commonly experienced phenomenon amongst the body of Christ. Therefore, this will not be a lengthy chapter. I largely wish to convey what the wilderness is, why it exists, and what can be gained from it.

The most prominent examples in Scripture of wildernesses, are, of course, Moses and the Israelites and Jesus Himself. We can draw some important conclusions from these two examples, as well as from individuals like David and various Old Testament prophets.

One important feature of a wilderness season is that it is initiated by God. Unlike the sifting discussed in the previous chapter, a wilderness season is begun and designed by God Himself. It was God who told Moses to bring the Israelites out of slavery and into the desert. It was the Holy Spirit who led Jesus into the wilderness to be tested. As in the case of David, it may not always appear to be initiated by the Lord (he entered the wilderness while fleeing for his life from King Saul), but the fruit of wilderness seasons is undeniably divine.

One of the typical features of the wilderness season is that it occurs in a time of transition from one chapter of life to another. For the Israelites, there was a transition from slavery to freedom. For Jesus, there was a transition from relative anonymity to His entrance into full-time public ministry. For David, there was a transition from living as a warrior in service to another to becoming a king. Most believers, I think, will concur that their experiences of wilderness seasons have often taken place at the closing of one era of life and before the beginning of the next. Why?

Why do we seem to enter into seasons of great hardship, loss, or difficulty between assignments and life stages? I believe the simple answer is preparation. God has called His people to live from glory to glory. Each new assignment, each new journey we begin with the Lord will require a formerly unknown level of character strength, maturity, obedience, and faith from us. We do not remain stagnant if we are truly pursuing the Lord. This means we are always being prepared for something greater, and usually more difficult, than the season we have left.

Because of this need for greater preparation, the wilderness season often involves significant loss. Many times there is loss of career, ministry, and financial stability. Even more painfully, wilderness seasons often involve the loss of relationships that have been significant to us in the previous chapter of life. Wildernesses nearly always require us to leave behind the things that were good and needed in the previous season but would hinder us in the season to come.

In a wilderness season, we will often come face-to-face with where we have allowed ourselves to become complacent, comfortable, or too dependent upon the blessings from the previous chapter of life. We will likely discover where we have allowed stability to replace faith in our hearts, where we have stopped relying on the Lord and begun relying on our steady income, our wealth of friends, or our own status and reputation. We will be shaken out of the creeping acceptance of mediocrity that tends to follow success and prosperity.

The wilderness also tends to cause us to confront areas in our lives that have never truly been dealt with, never fully healed, never entirely matured. We often find ourselves facing situations that trigger our deepest wounds, prod our sensitive areas, poke at our hidden fears, and finally get us to recognize that we need more healing, more deliverance, and even more growth. We often find ourselves faced with our biggest temptations in order to finally discover the roots of them. This is all in preparation for the next, higher level of things to come. But be assured, it is not comfortable or painless. There is suffering to be had, and plenty of it.

In a recent wilderness season of my own, within the span of a few weeks, I went from holding a leadership position in my church, heading a Christian school connected with that church, leading worship, heading a prison ministry, teaching, running spiritual trainings, having stable income, a large circle of acquaintances and even a few friends to having no income, no church, no job, no ministry, no friends, no acquaintances that I saw on any sort of regular basis, and no sense of what to do next. I lost the closest relationships I had in my life, hard-won financial stability, and the ongoing and daily involvement in the very things that I knew I had been created and called to do. Some of these things were my choice to leave behind because I knew God was calling me into a season of separation and isolation with Him. By some of them, however, I was completely blindsided. Some things that I was confident would be in my life no matter the season suddenly disappeared. I suddenly had no one and nothing but the Lord and my own children.

You may be able to imagine the pain and difficulty I experienced in this season. Many of you will not need to imagine it. Many of you have already been through this kind of wilderness. You may, at times, like me, have found yourself wishing, longing for how things were not so long ago, just as the Israelites found themselves longing for the meat and the produce of Egypt.

I have heard it said that you cannot shorten your wilderness seasons, but you can certainly lengthen them. There is something, or perhaps a number of things, specific things, that God desires for you to gain from your wilderness experience. Healing, growth, deliverance, and maturity in very specific areas are all packed into a much shorter time period than it would normally take to gain such growth. If we buck against the wilderness, if we go around rebuking Satan, convinced we are being attacked by him, if we waste our time looking back and wishing for the past season like Lot's wife, we will cause our wilderness to extend. The Israelites took a forty-day journey in the desert and managed to turn it into a forty-year ordeal before the nation was cleaned out of its idolatry, rebellion, immaturity, and slave-mindedness. At every opportunity, they looked for short cuts to arrive at the next chapter of life besides the way that God had laid before them.

I can tell you very sincerely that I have no desire to remain in any wilderness a single day longer than God intends me to be there. And so, in this wilderness, I decided to take the other path. I leaned into the wilderness with all my might. I asked God regularly, often daily, to show me the things I still needed to address, show me the wounds that needed healing, the immaturity that needed growth, and the strongholds that needed to be torn down. With each new loss, I grieved with Him with all of my heart, holding nothing in, allowing no foothold for bitterness or unforgiveness. I dug into the pain. I sat with it. I held it in my hands and stared at it until it had had its say and faded into impotence. Many things I faced in that wilderness were long-standing and could not come with me into the next season. Places where I did not know I had pride, where I did not see I lacked faith, where I was unaware of my own biases and weaknesses, all came to the surface to be scraped away. And I came away the better for it.

This book is a product of that wilderness.

If there is one piece of advice I could give anyone going through the wilderness right now it would be this: Don't run from the pain. Embrace it. Dig into it. Ask God what you need to learn from it, and learn it as quickly and as fully as you can. Many a powerful man and woman of God was birthed in the wildernesses of life.

I have never heard one of these individuals declare that such a time of intense trial and suffering resulted in ultimately less faith, less power, or a diminished relationship with the Lord. I have heard many of them claim just the opposite. Such suffering produced in them the very settled and immovable faith required to carry out the missions in which they currently walk. The fruit of such trials within those wholly determined to follow the Lord is good. Hard, but good.

CHAPTER 21

In their hearts humans plan their course,
but the Lord establishes their steps.

—Proverbs 16:9

There is another type of suffering I have encountered that I'd like to discuss here. It is a type of suffering we do not exactly bring upon ourselves, but our experience of suffering from it is wholly based on our own expectations. Often this type of suffering involves plans we had laid out for ourselves, dreams we intended to accomplish. It could be a job, a ministry, a certain number of children, or a spouse by some specific age. It could be a house, a school, an entrepreneurial venture, or someone you were certain was "the one." Whatever it may be, the main point is that it does not happen, or at least not on our prescribed timeline.

I have had many such experiences. Dreams, goals, relationships, life plans, and finances have all fallen through for me at various points throughout my life.

I explained in an earlier chapter about my career goals that were completely derailed by illness and physical incapacity. As I mentioned, the illnesses themselves were an intense point of suffering, but the loss of my dream was nearly as equally distressing, if not more so. The loss of something we've expected or long desired to take place is its own sort of torment. Sometimes we were convinced incorrectly that the thing was of God, only to discover that God was never in it. Sometimes it *was* God, but the decisions or actions of others prevented it from taking place. Sometimes it was God, but it was not for now. Sometimes it was God, but our own decisions and heart posture interrupted the very thing we desired and prevented it from taking place—the very thing God wished to give us. Whatever the situation, the disappointment of such experiences is palpable and often deeply felt.

The process for recovering from the pain of such suffering is often the same or nearly the same as it is for all suffering. Feel and process your emotions and disappointment in a healthy way. Forgive anyone who you need to forgive, align your heart to God's voice, and begin to prepare for the next chapter, taking any learned lessons with you.

However, I would like to point out briefly that, while there is not much we can do differently in recovering from this type of suffering, there is much we can do to prevent ourselves from experiencing it in the first place. Now, I do not think it's always completely avoidable. It is part of being a responsible human adult to plan for the future, and it is completely within the boundaries of healthy human emotion to begin feeling excitement, anticipation, and even some amount of emotional attachment to certain ideas and goals. But I am convinced that a great portion of the disappointment that believers feel from this brand of difficulty is not only completely unnecessary, but it's totally preventable.

A great example of this is what appears to be one of the most commonly experienced circumstances by young-adult believers in this arena. It is the search for a spouse. The number of people I have known who have stated that they were certain God had told them that So-and-So was "the one," their future spouse, their God-ordained destiny, is astounding—staggering, really. More often than not, this absolute confidence in their belief was based on nothing more than a dream they'd had, an off-handed statement by the person or by a mutual friend, a sense that they were called to be together. The number of individuals I've known who have found deep disappointment at the end of this road vastly outnumbers those who have not. You see, this is not a sustainable or functional way of determining your path to marriage, nor in life, nor with the Lord in general.

Human beings are infinitely capable of confirmation bias—a situation in which people suddenly begin to see evidence all around them to support the very thing they desire to be true. I have experienced this phenomenon in so many areas of my life it is difficult to tally them up. I have been convinced that God has called me to certain jobs, relationships, and geographical locations, and found plenty of "confirmations" to support the claim in each case. Some of these turned out to be accurate direction from God, and many others did not. The disappointment inherent in many of these situations was helpful in assisting me to learn the difference between God's voice and my own, but it did not often lead to joy or fulfillment in the moment. If the thoughts, longings of your heart, and plans for your future are all based on another person, you will begin to see "signs" everywhere that someone who fits your idea of a good spouse is "the one" for you.

I have known people who claimed that when they walked by and smelled the other person's brand of cologne on a random passerby, it was a sign from God that the person was the one for them. I have known people who have claimed that seeing some of the digits of a person's phone number on a license plate was a "confirmation" from God that the person was "the one" for them. More often than not, this belief began with a dream—a realm of spiritual communication the nature of which is almost always metaphoric or symbolic. A person who appears in your dream rarely represents themselves, even if the dream is spiritual in nature. But let's not forget that many dreams are created by our own emotions attempting to work themselves out while we sleep. Other dreams are nothing more than random bits of information that our brains are trying to defragment while at rest. And still others are wholly demonic in nature.

I will happily go on record as stating that God speaks to us in dreams, but this should rarely, if ever, be the only means of Him communicating important, life-altering direction to us in an area where we are so prone to see whatever fits our own emotional biases and desires. Dreaming is one part of a magnificently connected network of communication methods the Lord uses to speak to us. If you do not have the kind of ongoing, consciously aware spirit-to-Spirit interaction with the Lord that allows Him to communicate important information to you during prayer, worship, lunch, a shower, grocery shopping, and while making a sandwich, then developing an ongoing relationship should be your first priority before searching for a spouse.

It is a terrible, harmful, and manipulative means of beginning a relationship to use only a dream as the basis to inform someone that "God told me you are the one." It is equally as harmful to tell a person that God has told you they are "the one," even if your basis for that belief is stronger than a dream or an intense longing. Even if you don't speak it to them but instead sit and wait, hoping they will see it too, this is also manipulation. God has made us to be powerful individuals who are capable of and responsible for having open, genuine, powerful conversations with one another where one person shares their hopes and desires, and the other person is free to make decisions based on having all of the necessary information. Expecting God to keep giving you "signs" that a person is "the one" instead of, frankly, growing a pair and asking them out on a date to see if the two of you are on the same page or even compatible, is a system based on manipulative control at best. People set themselves up for absolute disappointment in such a system. Either you are devastated when the other person ultimately marries someone else (often having had no idea that you were interested in them in the first place), or when you marry this person you've been unhealthily obsessing over for months or years of your life, you're devastated when they turn out to be nothing more than another human being trying to make their way through life at best, or sometimes, a person with whom you are utterly incompatible.

The grief I have felt over Christian women I've known who have obsessed over some man being "the one" for large portions of their prime dating years, only to ultimately marry the man and find him to have nothing more than the technicality of salvation to offer as a spouse, is nearly unbearable. These women have often then been stuck in joyless, disconnected, and sometimes abusive relationships with the husband who they were so certain was "the one" for them. Who do you suppose takes the blame for that debacle? Generally, it is God to whom it is handed when He had nothing whatsoever to do with it. You see, it is not only those who don't get their spouse who have found great disappointment at the end of this road. A great number of those who have gotten their spouse this way live out their lives in relative unhappiness, often required to give up their dreams and callings in an attempt to make their marriage "work."

All this because we have set ourselves up to be fulfilled by the blessings God can give us rather than by the Giver Himself. All this because we insist on attaching our hearts to places, things, people, and ideas, more than to the One who created our heart and those things.

If there is one thing I like to think I've learned in this life, it is to hold every single thing with an open hand. I do my best to make plans based on any direction I believe God has given me. Certainly, God wants and expects us to become mature and powerful enough to make decisions based on the wisdom and understanding He has given us rather than always waiting for a specific directional word from Him. But I have come to tell Him time and time again that, at any moment, should He choose to tell me a new direction, that is all I need. I will give up any job, any house, any city or nation; I will give up any possession, any person, any ministry, any dream. There is nothing I have in my life that, if He asked me to give it up, I would not give Him. I believe this to be true. I hope I am never proven wrong. There is a small number of those things that I would have to grieve extensively in the process of relinquishing. Everything else is a *yes* without thought.

The fewer the things that have my heart's affection outside of God Himself and the people He has given me to love and the things I know He has given me to carry, the immeasurably less is the unneeded disappointment I feel when faced with unexpected change or the loss of one of these things. I know God loves to bless me. He has done so more than I could accurately recount. I also know that more often than not, His blessings are nothing like the blessings I wanted. They are infinitely better, sweeter, and more fulfilling than anything on which I had set my own heart.

There was a time after my divorce when I dated a man in my church. We were close in age and in similar life stages. It appeared to have potential. Many factors seemed compatible. He was certain that God meant for us to marry, which should have been my first red flag. However, I was fairly new to the healing process and still had much to learn about wisdom and discernment of human character. I spent well over a year feeling that I enjoyed his company, but I could not make a definitive statement about the future. There were things along the way that gave me pause, things that made me question his level of maturity and growth, but my uncertainty was much deeper than that.

Finally, after some time, I made a decision that I would give it a try; I would imagine my future with him and see what happened. I had been on a healing journey and was hoping that my newly won victories had given me some wisdom in making life decisions and that maybe this relationship could be something more. I allowed myself to open my heart to him in ways that I had previously held back. I began to make plans for the future that involved him.

One morning, I woke up with a heavy burden regarding this man. I had thought that stepping off the fence and going into this relationship would provide me more certainty about my path forward. It had not, and I began to realize that I was not, perhaps, far enough along in my journey of maturation to make such a decision wholly on my own. I did not want to step outside the path God had for me in one direction or another, so I asked Him. "God, I want to make decisions that are in line with whatever it is You've called me to do in the future. I don't want to turn down a blessing from You, and I also don't want to accept something that will hinder my ability to follow You anywhere You want to lead me. Please, tell me what I should do. I'm not healed enough or mature enough yet to see things as clearly as I want to. Please give me direction." It sounds like a simple statement, but it was a deep, burdened cry of my heart. Having come out of an abusive ten-year relationship with my ex-husband, I knew I wanted nothing to do with something that was not God's best for me, and I also knew I wasn't as healed as I had hoped, so my judgment could be off.

Looking back, I can see that had I been surrounded by a wonderful community of loving, mature believers who knew me and cared about me, I likely would have been advised to use caution. Having had very little opportunity for deep spiritual community in my life, I do not think it can be overvalued. It is essential for the growth process, as well as the healing process. I was, however, not in a church that was particularly mature or discerning in culture and had very few authentically loving people from whom to seek advice. So, for most of my spiritually awakened life, I have had to piece together a patchwork of people, often across the globe, to whom I can go for spiritual guidance. So, when I desperately asked the Lord for direction on this issue, it was with the full knowledge that I was highly unlikely to find a healthy, safe person in my own life to ask for guidance.

I rolled over in my bed and looked at my phone. A friend of mine to whom I hadn't spoken in some months had sent me a link to a video of a preacher I occasionally watched. I clicked on it, and the entire message was about it being time to give up Ishmael and prepare for Isaac; it was time to give up the thing that we want to be the right thing so God can actually bring the promise into our lives. While I was listening to this sermon, I felt a strong sense that this was God's answer to my question.

It happened to be a Sunday morning, and I walked out to my living room, still in my pajamas, and turned on a live-streaming church service of a church I often watch online. This church is totally separate and unconnected to the pastor whose sermon I had just finished watching. The sermon at this church on this day happened to be about how God was speaking to many in the body of Christ that it was time to set Ishmael aside and prepare to receive Isaac.

Alright, Lord, I thought. *I understand.*

A few days later, I was watching a Sunday sermon from yet a totally different and unrelated church to either of the first two. The speaker at this church was giving a message that I will never remember, and it had nothing whatsoever to do with my situation. The one thing I do remember is that in the middle of this message, he stopped what he was saying, looked at the audience, and said, "You don't marry Ishmael." He then looked confused and said, "I don't know why I just said that."

I do, I thought.

And so, I began the process of disconnecting my life from this man. It was painful, much more painful than it would have been prior to opening my heart to him. I had begun to form dreams, plans, and ideas for the future. I had become used to certain aspects of having someone in my life. As it turned out, the process of ending the relationship brought to the forefront in him the very types of character issues I had desperately wished to avoid in any future partner. I was so thankful that the Lord had been so clear with me. The ending was emotionally painful, but I could quickly see why the answer had been *no*. I shudder to think what my life would have been had I decided I was unwilling to give up a person to whom I was emotionally attached when the Lord said to do so. I had done that very thing once before, and a decade of abuse had followed. No matter how painful, I was determined to not make the same mistake again. I learned my lesson the hardest of ways. When the Lord says *no*, it is never to keep us from joy or happiness. It is always to preserve us from harm or keep us for something greater than what we desired.

When a relationship ends, there are two types of grieving: you grieve for the person themselves, and you also grieve for the dreams you had begun to build involving them, the hopes you had for the future. One particular evening after ending this relationship, I was grieving heavily, not for the person, but for the dreams and hopes to which I had begun to be attached. I sat sobbing on my couch after my children were in bed for the night. Ugly, snotty tears covered my face and clothing. Finally, I demanded of God, "So, what is it? Do You want me to be single forever? Am I just going to spend the rest of my life alone? Is that Your big plan for me?"

He asked me a simple question.

"If you knew that ending this relationship meant you'd be single for the rest of your life, would you turn back? Would you choose to stay in the relationship?"

Instantly I said, "No. Where else would I go, Lord? You have the words of life," repeating Peter's words when Jesus asked the disciples if they would also leave Him because of something that was difficult to accept. I didn't even need to think it over. The *no* was resounding and without hesitation.

It was shocking, and it completely derailed the self-pity that had crept into my grieving process. I stopped crying instantly and thought, *I wouldn't change a thing. If I knew that I would be single and alone for the rest of my life, there is still no possibility that I would make a different decision. He said to leave Ishmael behind, so, leave him I will.*

One of the most shocking parts of this experience was the fact that only a few short years before this, I would have struggled even to consider giving up a person to whom I had developed an emotional attachment. I had lived for so long in a state of connection poverty that the thought of relinquishing any connection I had managed to form was unable to be borne. A few short years before this, if I had managed to say *yes* to the Lord and leave this relationship behind it would have involved months, years even, of desperately brokenhearted despair and loneliness. But more than likely I would have found myself incapable of actually giving the thing up to begin with. The fact that my yes was so quick, my response to His question so instantaneously without thought or consideration was the surest sign of my healing I had yet seen. The years I had spent suffering the disappointment of lost dreams and desires had prepared me for excruciating pain in the midst of separating from a relationship. It was not excruciating, however. It was painful, but not having slipped nearly so far into the territory of building my hopes on a person rather than on the Lord as I had many times in the past, it was a short period of grief. I did truly grieve, but having built my hope on something far greater than a man, I was not knocked off my feet by it. I was able to maintain hope in the midst of grief to a degree previously unknown to me.

Now, as I write this, I do not have some grand story about an amazing husband who showed up on my doorstep immediately afterward. But I do have a massive amount of healing that took place directly after I was willing to let go of the relationship. I do have shifted circumstances in my life that have dramatically benefited my children and myself and positioned us for any number of things in the future. I don't know that in this case "Isaac" has anything to do with an actual man, and I'm certainly not banking on it. What I do know, is that "Isaac" is my promise. Whether this means greater and even deeper healing, stepping out into callings and authority previously unknown to me, or working in ministries that have long been on my heart, I don't know. But I'm absolutely convinced Isaac will be greater than Ishmael. This has already been the case, even before anything obvious and notable has taken place in my life. I am a different human than I was before this experience, as seems to be the case with all things God asks us to relinquish to Him. We are fundamentally changed in the giving, through the suffering of the giving.

You see, to look at God and say, "My answer is yes, no matter how much it hurts, no matter how much I really wanted this thing, my answer is always yes. It is always, 'Not my will, but Yours be done,'" cannot help but change the very fabric of who we are, the very nature within us. It is not an easy thing. It is hard. It is a hard road you have to choose, but the choice is more than worth it. If you never receive the thing you wanted, and even if you never receive something in its place, the new depths of the presence of God Himself into which you can enter because of slaying that idol are worth every moment of pain. The transformation into someone who is able to bear even more of the weight of His glory is well worth the suffering.

My hands were not quite as open as I would have wished in that moment, but when He asked me to, I opened them. There have been a number of times when I have needed to metaphorically pry those hands open through gritted teeth and screams of pain. In other situations, letting go of things God asks us to give up and waiting for things that we hope for, only to have them fall through, can test us. If we can actually have faith in those moments—not the kind that worries and strives in the meantime, but the kind that can simply trust that whatever God has for us is better than anything we have for ourselves—we will receive the promises of God. Not necessarily the things we hung our hopes on, but the things the One we should have hung our hopes on has for us, which are infinitely better.

And so, my admonition here to believers would be this. Do not build your life around the expectation of specific blessings. Build your life around the person and the presence of God Himself. If you find yourself thinking now of something, someone, or some situation that you don't think you could give up if God asked it of you, you can be sure that you've found an idol—something that's taken His place in your affections. I can assure you, anything God asks you to relinquish is nothing in comparison to what He will give you after you have done so. And if you find yourself unable to believe that God could give you anything as perfectly suited to you as the thing you don't want to give up, then I would say you haven't yet learned to trust Him, which indicates you do not know Him all that well. Because if you truly know Him, you cannot help but know that He is good, that the plans He has for you are good, and the blessings He reserves for you are good—better than anything you can think or imagine.

If you don't have that level of trust yet, then put Him to the test. If you believe He has asked you to give up a dream, a person, a situation to which you had become emotionally attached, do it and see if He doesn't utterly transform you in the process. I can tell you there has been little in my life so transformative as handing over to the Lord things that were within my power to hold tight. His presence, His glory, if it is the only prize, is prize enough.

CHAPTER 22

Learn to do right; seek justice.
Defend the oppressed.
Take up the cause of the fatherless;
plead the case of the widow.

—Isaiah 1:17

There is yet another brand of suffering to examine in regard to preventable pain. Unlike the suffering brought out in the previous chapter, this particular flavor of suffering is entirely brought upon us by our own action, or often, lack thereof. The type of suffering I am referencing here is that of conflict avoidance.

There seems to be an epidemic of conflict avoidance in our culture at this time, and its consequences have been disastrous. As someone who has been in leadership roles in both professional and ministerial capacities, I cannot tell you the number of people who have been shocked when I've actually brought to their attention an area of either job performance or character development that needed addressing. I have often been met with great offense and a nearly impenetrable wall of indignation when attempting to make simple and clear communication to individuals under my leadership about ways in which their actions were not aligned with the mission of the organization or the heart of God to our best understanding of it.

Now, keep in mind, as an autistic person, I have been made painfully aware that simple and straightforward communication, which comes first nature to me, is often considered unacceptable and "mean" in modern culture. While I do not claim to have perfected the art of diplomatic communication, I can assure you that our society is not benefiting from the attitude of "How dare you confront me about legitimate issues!" The church is most definitely garnishing no benefit from a culture of quick offenses and long grudges. It has led to a scenario where much of the global church is half individuals who cannot tolerate correction of any kind and another half who are so terrified of confrontation that they avoid it at all costs.

Each of us would do well to check ourselves in the area of correctability. It is not easy or pleasant for anyone who is less than truly healed and made whole in Christ, but we must be people capable of hearing where we need to grow, especially from others who care for us and have had the courage to bring their concerns to our attention. This doesn't mean we must listen to every critical voice that floats our direction. It simply means we absolutely must allow there to be voices that don't inherently share the exact same perspectives as our own in our lives. Can we receive correction and feedback from healthy, mature people? Is there anyone from which we are willing to hear about ourselves and the effects of our actions and decisions on the world around us? We must allow ourselves to have mirrors in other humans.

Becoming unoffendable is essential to a believer's life, however, this is not the topic of this chapter or book. Instead, I would like to point out the real and tangible suffering that we allow full access to our lives and the lives of those entrusted to our care: allowing our fear of other people's reactions to prevent us from confronting darkness, immaturity, or simple misunderstanding when, where, and with whom it is our responsibility to do so.

You will notice that I did not say whenever or wherever we meet with it, because, of course, it is not always our responsibility to confront others even when we see things well deserving of correction or confrontation. As a pastor's kid growing up, every person in my father's congregation seemed to believe that it was their responsibility to find and bring correction to any and everything they saw as having fallen short in my life. I can confidently assert that not one of them held a place in my life where it was appropriate for them to do so, and it caused much more damage than any benefit they'd hoped to bring from it.

However, a part of working through our fear of confrontation and conflict is to be able to recognize when it is, in fact, our responsibility to take action and when it is not. If you can realize that you will come across many more situations where it is not your responsibility or your right to confront than situations where it is, you may feel just a bit less intimidated by the thought of confrontation.

This is not an exhaustive discussion of this topic, but here are some general guidelines to assist in your recognition of when the burden is on your shoulders to take action to confront another person.

1. When the actions of another person have had a directly negative impact on you or someone who is under your care or protection (if that person is not in a position or of an age to engage in confrontation themselves), and those actions do not appear to be aligned with biblical principles or the heart of the Lord.

2. When the actions of another person have had a directly negative effect on a ministry, organization, or environment for which you carry some level of responsibility (such as being in a leadership role in your job or church), and those actions do not appear to be aligned with biblical principles, the heart of the Lord, or the values of that organization.

3. If the person whose actions are harmful or not aligned with the heart of God has invited you into a place of intimacy in their lives from which you have the right and responsibility to speak into situations involving them.

As I stated, this is not necessarily an exhaustive list, but a general guideline. The significant thing to note here is that the greater the level of authority we carry in any given environment, the greater the responsibility we have to confront wrongdoing when we encounter it. Though the Bible is clear that those who desire leadership roles desire a good thing, I would caution anyone who believes themselves to be called into positions of leadership to deal with any lingering fears of conflict or confrontation now. Do not let it wait. Leaders in the Kingdom of God have no business fearing confrontation. The consequences of fearing necessary confrontation are always disastrous.

Instead, we must examine the real culprit in our fear of conflict. In the vast majority of cases, our fear of conflict and confrontation is rooted in a deep fear of rejection. We are afraid of someone becoming angry with us and thus rejecting us, so we would rather leave wrongs unaddressed than face the potential pain of rejection. We often fear that setting healthy boundaries will cause others to abandon or dislike us, so we don't confront situations in which we or others in our care are being taken advantage of, harmed, or otherwise mistreated. We are often more afraid of the loss of connection or admiration than we are of the devastating consequences of refusing to confront harmful actions in others. And they are devastating, truly.

As an example of this, I'd like to examine the story of Absalom, the son of David, found in the book of 2 Samuel. I once heard Kris Vallotton give an excellent sermon on this story, and it has stuck with me since.

David is a biblical character with whom I have a great deal in common. There are many heroic, worshipful, and emotionally distraught moments of David's life laid out in Scripture with which I identify deeply. Unfortunately, one of David's characteristics I have often found myself identifying with is his fear of confrontation and conflict.

I admit it may seem odd to lay accusations of fear of conflict at the feet of the king who was unafraid to take on the complete spectrum of the enemies of Israel. This included a solo fight with a giant while still a boy, ensuring for many generations that the nation would no longer be subjugated or oppressed by the surrounding kingdoms. How could David possibly have been afraid of conflict? He was, at his core, a warrior.

I would like to point out the distinct difference between conflicts of a physical nature and those of an emotional nature. If we have questions about whether or not David had deep emotional struggles, simply read the Psalms and those questions will be answered. It's not an uncommon case for individuals who appear fearless in the face of physical danger to crumple into heaps of terror at the prospect of emotional confrontation. I have known many strong "fearless" men who would rather take a literal bullet than confess to another human that their feelings had been hurt by a person's actions or words. I myself have very often found that I would prefer a good fistfight to an interpersonal conflict any day.

As it so happens, the evidence of the brave King David's fear of confrontation and conflict is on full display within the stories of his children found primarily in the book of 2 Samuel. One of David's sons, Amnon, rapes his own half-sister named Tamar—one of David's daughters. Amnon and Tamar were half-siblings, having different mothers, but Tamar had a full brother named Absalom. When Absalom hears of Tamar's rape, he is furious with Amnon, as any good brother would be. But he responsibly does not take justice into his own hands, but instead waits for legal, righteous justice for his sister to come from his father, King David. But David's response is to do nothing. There is not so much as a conversation recorded in Scripture between David and Amnon referencing the atrocity that he perpetrated against his own sister.

For two years, Absalom silently awaits any action by David to grant justice or retribution for his sister, for Amnon to be held responsible for her pain and sorrow, which at that time and in that culture also meant the destruction of any hope for her to marry and have a family of her own. But David will not confront Amnon, even though Scripture tells us he was furious over Amnon's actions. He appears to hope that after some time has passed, the issue will simply be forgotten or resolve itself quietly.

Absalom, in turn, becomes so frustrated with his father's inaction that, in the end, when legal avenues have failed him, he does take justice into his own hands. He kills Amnon for what was done to Tamar.

Now, as the story progresses, Absalom is banished from Jerusalem for his actions, but some time later is allowed to return without the privilege of speaking face-to-face with his father. But the hatred and resentment that Absalom had spent years growing in his heart toward Amnon for his action and toward David for his inaction did not die with Amnon. Absalom's entire perception of his father had shifted from a man on whom he could rely for righteousness and justice to a man who was unfit to lead a kingdom.

As a result, Absalom sets out on a campaign to turn the hearts of the people of Israel against David and toward himself. The Bible is clear that he was quite successful in this endeavor. He sat at the city gate telling those who would seek justice from the king that they would find no justice there. In his heart, I'm sure he believed this to be true. His own experience with David had taught him this.

Eventually, Absalom is successful in driving David out of the city and styling himself as the true king of Israel with the support of a great number of Israel's people. And he is successful for some time. Some of David's most mournful psalms were written during this period of exile. Now, Absalom had spent a great deal of time nurturing hate in his own heart—a destructive force causing him to commit atrocities that he would likely not have committed at a previous time in his life. Eventually, he is rightfully removed as king, and David is reinstated to continue his bloodline through his son Solomon.

I would like to point out, though Absalom was entirely responsible for the growing bitterness and hatred in his own heart toward his father, the seed of this hatred was placed there by David's avoidance of confrontation. He was willing to allow his own daughter to live for years with injustice, which is its own kind of trauma, his son to have years of frustration and pain grow into resentment and rage, and his daughter's rapist to go free with no consequences. This ultimately resulted in his son becoming a murderer, his kingdom being forcibly taken from him, many of his previously loyal men abandoning him, the rapes of his concubines, and a full-blown civil conflict in the land of Israel. There are many consequences listed beyond these to innumerable individuals within David's kingdom that can be read in the account in Scripture. All this so that David could avoid a painful conflict with his son. It, perhaps, gives us a clue into how Amnon developed into the kind of man who would forcibly harm his own sister in the first place. David was, arguably, the best king Israel ever had. He was, however, by all appearances, a poor father. Even his son Solomon, one of the only other real candidates for the title of the greatest king in the history of Israel, gives the credit for his wisdom to his mother in the book of Proverbs, not to his father.

Had David dealt justly and swiftly with Amnon, Absalom would have likely fostered feelings of gratitude, honor, and loyalty to his father for his righteous handling of a painful circumstance. Instead, David's avoidance of conflict ruined countless lives, ended many lives, and resulted in broken relationships with his children.

In our process of maturing in Christ, we must address this utterly destructive pattern that has taken up residence within many of us. It's the lie that we are being Christlike if we avoid conflict. We are not. Our self-preservative mindset of conflict avoidance is not only not Christlike, it is incredibly damaging to ourselves and others and creates a mountain of unnecessary suffering. Let's remind ourselves that Christ flipped tables in the temple and drove out the money changers with whips. He called the Pharisees *children of the devil* to their faces and challenged them openly and publicly on their hypocrisy and sin. Being both God and the promised Messiah, it was His right and responsibility to do so. We are not being Christlike if we do not take the initiative to confront people and situations that are our responsibility to confront. We are being cowards. Cowardice invariably leads to suffering. As the famous quote states, "The only thing necessary for the triumph of evil is for good men to do nothing." If there is one thing that I know Jesus was not, it is a coward. So, as His followers, we have no business being cowards while evil and dysfunction are given free reign around us. No ministry, no family, no relationship can survive where confrontation is not permitted.

Is confrontation frightening? Certainly. Is there a likelihood of rejection by those we confront or those with whom we have conflict? A high likelihood in our current culture. I have lost more than one relationship with people who I truly loved because of the desire to bring to light and resolve areas of behavior that were not in line with the Word of God or His heart, and these were people who there was a clear responsibility for me to address about difficult topics. Does this excuse us from engaging in conflicts that are necessary for growth or the execution of righteousness? No, it does not. I have lost count of the church splits I've witnessed in my life, splits that were easily preventable if a righteous leader had been willing to address a small issue at an early stage instead of waiting for it to become a large issue down the road. The body of Christ has no right to live in fear.

This is not a judgment on those who experience fear of conflict. My own brain was wired to be terrified of conflict for as far back as I have memory. It has been a long and harrowing journey to step out of the fear and develop the capacity to confront darkness in other humans and in situations with as much love and truth as I am able to utilize. I still often feel fear when approaching conflict and sometimes still struggle to convince myself to engage in the conflict to begin with. But it is necessary to place that fear where it belongs: nowhere near my decision-making process, and, eventually, altogether gone.

This is a requirement for leadership. This is a call to arms. We must become ruthless with our fear. We must get healed in the places where we fear rejection more than unrighteousness and its consequences. We cannot become the whole and complete body of Christ until we've lost our fear of addressing sickness and disease within the body.

One thing I have learned is that ignoring something invariably does not cause it to vanish; it usually causes it to multiply. If fear is a type of "faith" (faith in darkness) as it appears to be, and if faith is a force that shifts things in the direction of whatever we place our faith in, then fear of rejection will always ultimately lead to the destruction of human relationships. Let's save both ourselves and those in our lives from a great deal of unnecessary suffering by confronting the first thing in this scenario that requires confrontation: our own fear.

Forgiveness and Greater Understanding

CHAPTER 23

*Then Peter came up and said to him,
"Lord, how often will my brother sin against me, and I
forgive him? As many as seven times?"
Jesus said to him,
"I do not say to you seven times, but seventy-seven times."*

—Matthew 18:21–22

One of the most important topics to cover in any discussion of suffering is forgiveness. Now, we know there are types of suffering that do not require us to forgive anyone at all, as well as some types of suffering that only require us to forgive ourselves. But I am specifically referring to the forgiveness of others who have caused us pain or distress.

This book was not written as a how-to manual for forgiveness and healing, though I hope you have found some helpful insights into these topics. What I will do is briefly tell you why I believe forgiveness is so crucial to the healing process and share with you my own journey of forgiveness for the people who have been the most difficult for me, personally, to forgive.

In essence, forgiveness is the process of letting go—releasing. I have heard many people say that in order to forgive, you must simply say over and over, as many times as it takes, that you forgive someone, that you choose to forgive, and eventually it will stick. I will not say they are wrong. This may very well work for some people or in some situations, and I do believe that there is an act of choice, of will, involved in the forgiveness process. But this method alone did not work for me for the deeply traumatizing experiences I had lived through at the hands of others.

I spent years choosing to forgive my parents, and yet, I never actually did forgive them. When I would see them, they could still trigger me to rage and trauma in a moment. If they did something I saw was wrong, I felt disgust for them. I believed myself to be better than them and was just waiting for the day when this fact would be undeniably proven to them and others. I hoped for other people to discover the truth of who they were behind closed doors. Why? Not because I wanted truth to win the day, but because I wanted them to be exposed, humiliated, and in all effects, smote—to be removed from their little thrones of control and get what was coming to them.

I recognized these feelings as wrong and tried to renounce them and declare them away at every opportunity. The only problem is while we have been given the authority to command both the realms of the spiritual and the physical, the realm of our own emotions (our soul) cannot be cast out, delivered, or even, generally speaking, healed on command. Forgiveness is a process, shorter for some people than for others, but it is always a process with very specific steps that must be taken in order for it to have any effect.

First, you must actually allow yourself to *feel* your emotions. This means you must acknowledge them, write them out, scream them out if you must. The (undelivered) letters I have written to people who have hurt me would make most good church attenders faint in horror. As Christians, we are often taught that it is wrong to be angry, it is wrong to think horrible things about another person, it is wrong to despise someone. Some of these statements do undeniably have truth in them. We are, after all, called to love our fellow humans with the love of Christ, and we are told in no uncertain terms that hatred is the equivalent of murder (1 John 3:15).

The problem is, our emotions don't particularly care about what is wrong or right, and they don't automatically line up with what our conscience says they should be. Now, I have known a great many Christian leaders who have given terrible advice about mastering your emotions. And while I don't believe we should allow ourselves to be slaves to our emotions or base our decisions solely upon them, they exist for a reason. And if you ignore, push down, and otherwise white knuckle through them until you've gotten yourself "under control," all you've really accomplished is, at best, a delay of those feelings. At worst, you've started a ticking time bomb that will eventually explode all over the people you love and leave you portraying a poor representation of the Kingdom of God on the earth in the explosion.

As a side note, self-control, often touted as the means by which emotions are to be stamped out, is not an act of will, primarily. It is a fruit of the Spirit (Galatians 5:23), meaning it's an automatic outgrowth of an internal existence where the Spirit reigns supreme. Additionally, I believe that self-control is meant to be a tool (acquired through intimacy with the Holy Spirit) used to place boundaries on our *actions*, not to control our emotions. The church has confused this information, promoting self-control as something that can be conjured up by mere force of will to be used to squash our (God-given) emotions.

You see, the problem is not the emotion. The problem is the thing that caused the emotion, namely pain. And until you have felt that pain, fully and completely, allowing it to exist in its entirety within you for as long as it takes, it will not disappear. You cannot force it away. There is not enough willpower in the world to make such a thing happen.

So, the first step in the process of forgiveness is to experience your own pain. Say, write, scream exactly what that person did to you, how it made you feel, and how much you hate them for it. Yes, that is what I said. If the goal is to no longer hate, we must first acknowledge that we do, in fact, often hate people for the pain they've caused us. The church often seems to want healing to be clean, proper, and wrapped up in a neat bow at the end. It isn't. It is messy, it is painful, it will tear your soul to pieces so that it can finally be put back together in its intended order. We must stop telling people to fear, hide, or be ashamed of their emotions. We must be authentic enough to accept that human beings, including ourselves, are complex beings woven all throughout with complicated emotional responses to our experiences.

Healing is never going to be proper. It's never going to be an experience we walk away from thinking, "That really showed my best side." It's time to get over that fact and *just do the thing*. If hatred resides in your heart toward someone, pretending it isn't there or blocking your own ability to consciously experience it does not put you in line with the command not to hate. It prevents you from doing so. If you squash your hatred toward a person who has harmed you and simply refuse to feel it in an attempt to be "righteous," you do not allow it any means of egress from your soul. It is stuck, trapped, and so are you. If you can be triggered to feelings of rage or hatred toward someone by circumstances or interactions with them, be assured that hatred toward them is resident within you. The fact that you do not walk around constantly feeling it does not indicate its absence. It only displays the fact that it's simmering under the surface rather than having been allowed to rise to the top where it might have been scraped away, removing the dross, and leaving only the silver behind. The only way to come into alignment with the command not to hate is to let the hatred finally work its way out.

I spent months writing my parents letters (that I will never give them) almost daily, filled with hatred, poison, foul language, and the worst intentions before the infection was finally purged. But it cannot be purged if we don't squeeze it out. Please, do yourself this favor: do not waste your time judging yourself in the middle of your healing process. Don't be horrified by your own emotions. Be grateful that you can access them and hopefully be healed of the pain that caused them.

Now, after having finally allowed myself months of feeling my deepest, ugliest emotions toward my parents, I felt a lot less angry, but I still didn't have anything resembling what you might call love in my heart for them. So, I knew I still had not forgiven them fully. Again, this may be a point where common advice might say to simply choose and declare that you release the person from all obligations and debts to you, that they owe you nothing, and you choose to let go of any expectation of recompense by them. These are all very good and important declarations, and again, there may be thousands of people who have found them helpful in their process. I'm sure some were truly launched forward in their forgiveness process by making these declarations, and I do think there is a point where they're needed. There is a point where our emotions, our will, and our ability have all lined up and our entire being can successfully make this decision, in which case, it will likely finally stick. However, when I first attempted to make such declarations, it seemed to have little or no effect on me whatsoever. I have since come to the conclusion that, at least for me, and at least for the types of violations for which I was attempting to forgive my parents, the only thing that makes a difference is a face-to-face encounter with the living God. It is only after such an encounter when I have found myself with the capacity to actually choose forgiveness with the entirety of my being.

I have learned and am learning to forgive many people. The most difficult for me were, obviously, my parents. The pain of the parental wounds I received from them was deep and long-standing. It reached back, not only to my earliest moments on this earth, but even to generations prior.

The rage I felt toward my father is difficult to adequately convey. I felt the man had failed me in every possible way. That was not exactly true. There are certainly worse things he could have done as a father than he did, and there were areas where he attempted to do what he believed was right for his children. I do not deny this. However, he did largely fail as a father in the sense that in the majority of his actions toward his children, he portrayed the very opposite of the love that our true Father has for us. Where the Father promotes freedom, my earthly father demanded control. Where the Father is slow to anger and abounding in love, my earthly father was quick to rage, and few, if any, of his children had a deeply held belief that he loved them. I could go on, but the purpose of this statement is to point out the great amount of pain for which I needed to forgive my father. But after weeks and months of feeling and purging my own emotions about him, it was difficult for me to even conjure up enough anger to write another letter.

"What do I do, now, Lord?" I asked. "I want to really forgive him, but I haven't. But I'm not sure I have anything left to write."

So, I did what I knew to do and pulled out my notebook and pen and once again began a letter to my father. To my astonishment, it turned out to be a letter that I may actually give him one day. The anger was largely done boiling over. The calm I felt replaced it, and I was finally able to begin to look at my father differently—not my failure of a father, but a man who had been horrifically traumatized in his own early life and had tried to be better than what he had experienced. He had not succeeded in many ways, but I was finally able to acknowledge the attempt to take his family line a small step or two forward. These are things I had previously been capable of acknowledging on an intellectual basis, but never emotionally.

As I wrote, the strangest thing began to happen. A love for my father I had never before experienced began to blossom in my heart. I thought it was my own love at first, but it quickly grew to an intensity that required me to acknowledge that no human being was capable of producing this great a love for another person. I began to weep uncontrollably out of sheer love for my father. I could see him as the little boy who was never given a moment of affirmation in his life, who desperately needed a father himself. I saw him too afraid to be vulnerable because he had never experienced what it was like to be emotionally safe. And I loved him exactly where and how he was.

The strangest thing about this love was that it required nothing from my father. It was not based on a hope that he would change or even that he was capable of it. It was not founded on a desire to have a reestablished relationship with him at some point in the future. There was nothing it sought in return from him. It was just love, given and given and given until I thought I might die from it. How could a human body contain such love? Mine felt as though it would tear apart at any moment.

If I decide to give the letter to my father at some point, I will likely have to rewrite it because the original is warped and streaked from the tears that soaked its pages.

I have had very little contact with my parents for some time, but on the occasions when I have seen them, it has been strange and utterly unexpected how peaceful I feel about interacting with my father. Since I am on the hunt for healthy human connections now, I don't know that I would seek him out for a relationship at this time, as he appears to be, essentially, the same person he always was. But I do not have any difficulty in being around him, conversing in a normal way. It is the oddest feeling to know that my father seems to no longer have the ability to trigger me. I have seen and heard him do some childish and inappropriate things since my encounter with the Lord, and frankly, I cannot even take them seriously. He is a little boy, after all—a little boy who God adores. Of course he will react to the world as a little boy would. Why would I expect something different?

Once you have truly forgiven someone, it is almost disorienting to be in proximity to them, no longer having any set pattern for your interactions to follow. My relationship with my father was always based on irritation at best and at worst, rage. Our interactions were laced with it at every turn. Now, there is no pre-established pattern to follow. It's as if he is a man I've just met for the first time, a stranger, and I can decide how near or far he will be in my life and how seriously I will take him. This is incredibly liberating.

Some time after this encounter with the love of God for my father, I was speaking with a mentor of mine about my own concerns as a parent. You see, while I have always known I love my children more than anything on this earth, I have been painfully aware of my missing skillset when it comes to parenting. I had very few moments resembling love in my childhood, no sense of acceptance, and zero validation of my emotions or experiences. There was not the slightest shadow of a path I could follow to understand how to parent my children in a way that would not lead to the destruction of their souls. And so, I have often felt as if I am blundering around in the dark, hoping I'm making the right decisions, praying I am finding some balance between building their identity and building their character. As I expressed these concerns to my mentor, he said something to me that broke open a new layer of understanding and forgiveness.

He said that if you think about parents as each having a deck of cards that their children need from them, things like identity, emotional availability, etc., you can learn to see parenting through a different lens. If your child needs five cards from you, he said, but your parents only gave you two, and you give those two to your children, then you are a good parent. If your parents gave you those two cards, but you only give your children one, then you are not a particularly good parent. But, he said, if you somehow manage to scrape together and produce a third card out of nothing and give it to your children, then you are an amazing parent because you only had two to give in the first place, but you gave them more. Even though they really needed five cards, you gave them everything you could and even more than you had.

I pondered this for some time, and it truly did change my perception of my own parenting journey. And after that, something else happened. I began to think about my father as a parent. Knowing what I knew about his childhood, I thought it likely he had entered his own parenting journey with maybe one card, if any. I definitely needed at least five from him, but he simply didn't have them to give. My mother on the other hand, I was certain, had probably set out to look for any cards I may have been born with to take those from me if she could.

But as I began to think back on my childhood, I remembered moments in my life where my father had deposited something in me, something of which I was only recently becoming aware. I remembered at different times when he had coached my soccer teams. He did not teach skills gently. He was forceful and often harsh. But even in the midst of his harshness, I began to see a dynamic at play without which I don't believe I would have come out of my childhood with even the capacity to heal.

You see, my father could not abide losing. Every team of mine he ever coached was either a championship or second-place team. And this was not simply because my teammates and myself were afraid of him. No, my father had "pulled himself up by his bootstraps" as the saying goes, for his entire life. He had never healed from his past wounds, certainly. But he had dug deep and found some strength that had, at the very least, turned him into a productive member of society rather than an addict or wastrel. He had fought and bled for everything he had in his life, and he expected this from the players he coached. He didn't just expect it, he inspired it. He didn't care about someone's skill level or how impressive they looked on the field. He cared if they put every ounce of

155

strength, force, and will they had (and then some more besides) into being first to the ball. When they lost the ball, he cared if they immediately turned and focused every molecule of power in their muscles on taking it back. He cared whether they stopped running, defeated, when a player from the other team got around them, or if, instead, they ran like the wind to stop the other team from reaching our goal before they scored.

We drilled, and we drilled, and we drilled. We perfected everything we could perfect, and we filled in the gaps with sheer brute strength and willpower. And we loved every moment of it. I was never so happy in my childhood as when I was on the soccer field and my dad was coaching on the sideline. If my father had a true calling in life, I suspect this was it. I can only imagine the feats he could have accomplished as a coach if he had been a healed man.

As I pondered this phenomenon, I realized my father had put me in touch with a part of myself that had lain cut off and dormant during my earlier childhood. The abuse and rage of my mother had made me terrified of everything. I fled from conflict as though my life depended upon avoiding it (I often thought it did). I hid, I was silent, I prayed not to be noticed. I felt weak, helpless, powerless.

But at my very first ever soccer practice (to which I was terrified to go), something came alive in me that never went back to sleep again. It was my own spirit. It was the warrior who knew what it meant to press through hardship, to conquer, to overcome, and it allowed my soul to learn the same skills. When I played soccer, my soul and spirit found a oneness that existed nowhere else in my life. I was strong, I was powerful. I could do this. I never developed much finesse in the sport or had fancy footwork or impressive moves, but one thing I could do was run head-first into a pack of boys twice my size and come out with the ball, most of them being left on the ground behind me. This I could do.

After thinking on this for some time, I came to the conclusion that my dad had given me one card. He had somehow managed to put me in touch with my own spirit, my heaven identity, without even intending to. He had awakened the fighter, the warrior, and as it turned out, this was, in fact, the only card I had needed to embark on a journey of finding the other cards for myself. This was the one, absolutely essential card that had to be in play in order for me to come out of my childhood with the ability to pursue healing and wholeness rather than sinking into life-long despondency or worse—narcissism like my mother.

I don't know if my dad had been given this one card somewhere by his own parents or another person in his life or if he had somehow managed to produce it out of nothing and hand it to me. But what this meant was that at worst, my dad was a good father. Although he gave me nearly nothing that I needed from him, he gave me what he had. And, as it turned out, it was enough. I don't diminish the harm he did to me throughout my life. I have had to face and feel more pain from that relationship on my healing journey than nearly any other. And yet, I can no longer help but see my dad, not just as the little boy that God loves with such intensity, but as a father, my father, who did good.

And this is what forgiveness accomplishes. Without my father having done one thing, the entire story of our relationship has been rewritten. There are scars now in places that not too long ago were open and infected wounds. And scars tell a story—the story of a God who can take any broken thing and make it whole, who can take any pile of ashes and make it beautiful.

CHAPTER 24

And when you stand praying, if you hold anything against anyone, forgive them, so that your Father in heaven may forgive you your sins.

—Mark 11:25

My journey of forgiveness for my mother was a bit more difficult. Even after the encounter I had with the Lord where He showed me the choice I had made to take on this assignment in my life, there was so much hatred, rage, and malice caged up in my heart toward my mother. I thought it was impossible for me to ever reach a place of total forgiveness.

I had encounters with the Holy Spirit where She showed me truly and tangibly what the love of a mother was. She returned to me my dignity and honor and told me things that my heart had been longing for a mother to tell me for as long as I could remember. It healed so many places within my soul. Yet, I still couldn't seem to forgive my mother.

I also knew that I had long dealt with a continuous feeling of being superior to her. She was evil, pure and simple from my perspective. My mother lived to torment, harm, and manipulate people. I was not this. Yes, I had hurt people in my life, I knew, but it had not been my intention. It had been the result of deep and ugly brokenness, but I had never thrived on making others suffer. I was disgusted with her. She was beneath me. I was better than her and couldn't wait for her to get what was due her. I recognized this as pride but could not seem to rid myself of it. After all, I was objectively a better mother, Christian, human being than she was. The things she had done to me were so far removed from any thought that had ever entered my mind that I felt as if we were almost different species. And my species was superior.

Finally, one night, I lay on my living room floor and said, "Holy Spirit, I need more information. If I am going to forgive my mother, I need to understand things about her like I did with my father, to see her how You see her."

So, I began asking the Holy Spirit questions about my mother. It was a simple line of questioning. I knew my assignment had been to break the bloodline curse in her family and that generations before me were supposed to have completed this task but did not. This left me feeling as though I had to bear the weight of all of their weakness and failure. *How unfair.* I rolled my eyes thinking about their weakness and failure. After all, I had never been so weak that I had to turn to narcissism as a coping mechanism, had I? What was wrong with her that she was so weak? I felt it was pathetic.

"Holy Spirit," I asked, "did she volunteer for this assignment too? Did she think she was strong enough to complete it and just found herself too weak to finish the job?"

"She didn't volunteer for this," was the simple answer. "She was asked."

I contemplated, letting the idea roll around in my head. After a few minutes, I began to feel a bit indignant.

"How could You do that?" I asked. "How could You ask her to break this bloodline curse, knowing she wasn't strong enough to do it?" In my heart, I was actually appalled by the idea, angry, in fact. God knew my mother was too weak to take on this assignment yet asked her to do it anyway?

"We didn't ask her to break the curse," She said solemnly. "We asked her to be a steppingstone so that you could break the curse." And with this statement, I saw an image of my mother stepping forward into a line of people. She fell face forward, and as she fell, she turned into a large, gray, stone disc that landed heavily on the ground, ready for my foot to stand on.

My world shattered.

I saw a vision of my mother in heaven before beginning her assignment on the earth. She was a gentle spirit with hopes for her future life. She dreamed of being a dancer, living out her calling to worship the Lord through dance in her earthly life. She looked the same age my spirit had when I saw myself prior to my life on earth—an older teen or very young adult.

I saw the moment when they asked her if she would be my steppingstone, if she would give up every dream she'd had for life to make it possible for me to cleanse that ugly, poisoned bloodline. The sadness, the disappointment she felt, I could not bear it. I began to weep as I understood the sacrifice she had made to lay a path for me to accomplish my mission.

Holy Spirit explained to me that my great-grandfather had so thoroughly and totally partnered with evil that there was not a human who could have survived what my mother went through and still had enough strength or enough time in one lifespan to break the curse. What they needed was someone who could suffer through the agony of what her grandfather did to her but not be as corrupt, not partner with evil as much as he had. They needed someone to dilute the curse enough to make it possible for the next person to break it. To go to earth, be brutalized, and brutalize the next generation to a lesser extent.

I wanted there to be a different answer, but I knew if there had been another way, the Lord would have taken it. Without violating people's free will, He is free only to work within the confines of what humans are both able and willing to do.

She said *yes*. It devastated her. But she said *yes*. I saw her set aside her dreams of dancing and lay down the hopes she'd had of a beautiful life. In the spirit, they were actual items that she could set down. And she did—a small pile of them on the ground beside her just before she stepped into the line of people. She said *yes* knowing that she would be tormented and abused, knowing she would cause unthinkable damage to others. It was nothing like she had hoped. But she said *yes*.

"Like a lamb to the slaughter," I said in dismay. "Like a lamb to the slaughter," I kept repeating in my head, the knowledge of it breaking my heart into a thousand tiny pieces that seemed to spill all over the floor.

I turned to the Holy Spirit. "Why did You send someone so gentle, so weak, to be brutalized so horribly?"

The sorrow in the answer is difficult to convey. And yet the answer was matter-of-fact as if there simply was no other option.

"No one could survive her grandfather," She replied. "We could not waste your strength in a situation that would ultimately destroy you. We needed it to break the curse. We needed someone who wasn't strong to be the steppingstone, someone who did not have strength to be wasted."

Then, my heart did really tear into pieces. I could feel it being ripped and shredded violently in my chest with the sorrow of this understanding. I grieved for her at least as deeply as I have ever grieved for myself, possibly more. The cries and screams of sorrow I wept for her came from a place deeper than any I had known, I suspect back to the depths of her own soul, if not generations even further back. You see, I was not just grieving my own sorrow for her. I was grieving *on behalf of her*. I was doing the grieving that she had never done for the suffering in her life. I suddenly had a deeply felt revelation that all suffering must be grieved, and if you do not grieve your own suffering, you leave it ungrieved for others to then carry until someone has grieved it. Likely it will be your children and their children until someone has touched the depths of pain that you experienced and grieved it out of your bloodline.

I was ruined. How could it be borne, this knowledge? How could it be carried? How could I wake up the next day and continue to live the same life I had lived previously?

Next, I saw my own spirit standing next to my mother's. I was in full battle armor, standing tall and strong. She was a gentle flower, blowing in the wind. There I was, a war-trained soldier, prepared for battle, ready to hack, slice, tear to pieces. There she was soft and beautiful, gentle and tender. The strength that had made me so prideful now made me appear clumsy, oaf-like, beastly.

"I'm like a bull in a China shop," I told the Holy Spirit. And I thought again about the sacrifice to which she had said yes.

Suddenly I could stand it no longer. I threw myself at the vision of my mother's feet and wept all the more.

"I am not better than you," I cried, sobbing. "You are better than me. You are better than me."

I did not know what true humility was until this moment, and I pray often that I will have the privilege of such perspective for every person with whom I come into contact in my life.

Holy Spirit then showed me a vision of my mother's soul.

I saw a little girl with brown hair in pigtails. She was wearing a yellow dress and had yellow ribbons in her hair. But she was trapped inside of a cage. This cage was not rectangular, but circular in shape. There were bars all around, and surrounding the exterior of this cage were feet and feet of dense, hard rock in every direction. She was encased in it. There was not one crack in the rock, not one tiny hole where something could slip in from the outside to reach her. She was in total darkness. She walked around and around the cage continuously, pulling on the bars, calling out, "Can anyone hear me? Is anyone there? Help me, please!" But nothing could get in, and nothing could get out.

I had a sudden realization. You see, I had long been bitter about a particular situation involving my mother. It had seemed for some time as though the Holy Spirit spoke to her quite frequently. She regularly had dreams, visions, and prophetic revelations. I often strongly disagreed with her interpretations of these experiences, but it was clear that they were legitimate encounters with the Holy Spirit. Having always struggled deeply with connecting with the Holy Spirit (presumably because of the mother issues that existed in my soul), it had seemed utterly unfair to me that, knowing the abuse and damage she had done to her children, the Holy Spirit would be so keen to communicate with her while I tried desperately to connect and often found what felt like silence.

"Is this why You speak to her so often in the spirit?" I asked, looking at my mother's barricaded little soul.

"Yes," She replied. I felt Her gentle affection for my mother. "I cannot reach her soul, so I speak to her spirit every chance I get." I could feel the depth of love and adoration communicated in that simple statement. The Holy Spirit adored my mother without hesitation, wholly unconnected to anything she had or had not done in her earthly life. In fact, I felt a particular fondness that the Holy Spirit had for my mother because of the sacrifice she had made. She had not been forgotten.

It brought to mind the verse in 2 Timothy that references vessels used for noble and ignoble purposes. My mother's assignment had been, in many ways, an ignoble purpose, and mine, what would be considered noble. However, I could recognize the ways in which I had been designed for just such a task. My tenacity, my stubborn refusal to permanently give up in the face of hardship, was not something I had created in myself; it was placed there by God. I could take no credit for it. I had been designed for just such a mission. My mother, however, had not been designed for a mission such as hers. She knew it would break her. And yet she willingly took it on. How could I have thought myself superior?

Whatever purpose, noble or ignoble, for which my mother and I had been sent to the earth, both were necessary. Both were absolutely essential to God's plans being fulfilled in this family line. I know that 2 Timothy 2:20 can be interpreted to mean that vessels for common use are of less value. It indicates that we should all pursue becoming vessels of gold and silver, vessels of noble purposes, and I believe that is accurate. But sometimes the floor must be scrubbed. Sometimes the batter must be stirred before it can become a cake, and so the scrub brush and the wooden spoon are equally as important as the golden plate or the silver utensils. Perhaps they are even more so, as the plates and utensils would hardly be necessary if there was no food to place on them—food made with the wooden spoon. The steppingstone is equally as necessary as the person who will step on it since that person cannot reach their destination without it.

Looking at her trapped soul, I could see what she had actually sacrificed to accomplish this ignoble, essential purpose.

I turned back to the Holy Spirit. "Can't anything be done?" I asked, tears streaming down my face.

"Not in this life. There isn't enough time left in her life to repair the kind of damage she has taken."

"What then?"

She pointed and I followed with my eyes. There I saw Jesus. He had built a house for my mother. It was waiting for her in heaven. I had always believed she was saved despite her brokenness, so I was not surprised to know that He had prepared a place for her. I was surprised by what the house looked like, however.

It was situated deep in a forest, far away from any other houses or people. It was placed at the foot of a mountain that was lush with deep green life all the way up to its top, miles and miles above. There were tall, dark green trees nestled into the sides of the house. It was a place of seclusion, of healing.

But there was one problem. The house was made of nothing more than bare cement. It was a one-room cement cube with a few squares cut out of its walls for windows and a doorway. There was no color, no actual door or windows, no decorations or embellishments of any kind, nothing of beauty, and the only item of furniture in the house was a spare little cot, upon which I saw my mother's spirit resting. She looked gray and sickly, and I knew that I was seeing what would take place when my mother reached heaven after her death. Her spirit was meant to recover in this home, in this sick bed, from all of the darkness of her life. But, while there was a building, there was no splendor in it, nothing in the house itself that might bring comfort, encouragement, or solace.

I asked the Holy Spirit what I was seeing. She told me, "Jesus did the best He could with what He had to work with." And I suddenly knew that He had built her house out of her salvation. The cement had been meant to form the foundation of her house, not the full structure. More should have been built upon it with all of the moments spent in real pursuit of the ways of God, in pursuit of God Himself. Jesus had stretched it far enough to give her a house, but nothing more. Her life had been consumed only with pursuing the praise of man and control of others, so there were no other treasures with which He could build.

I was overtaken in a moment by the deep conviction that such an outcome was wholly unacceptable, unjust.

"It's not good enough," I stated firmly, remembering the sacrifice she had made for me. "She said yes to that mission. She sacrificed all of her dreams, and this is all that's waiting for her at the end?" It is difficult to explain because this place was clearly heaven. It was made of the substance of heaven. There was not a drop of deficiency or sin present. This cement cube, made of salvation, was by far better than houses made by men here in this realm of the dying. But I was gripped with the conviction that it was not enough of heaven to make up for what she had done, what she had chosen, what she had given up.

"She had no other treasures to work with," the Holy Spirit reminded me gently. "Treasures are earned during a lifetime on the earth."

I turned to Jesus. "Take my treasures," I said resolutely, tears again pouring down my face. "Anything that is not absolutely and completely mine and needed for my house, take it."

I felt Jesus smile, and as I watched, the little house filled with furniture, a wooden table and chairs, windows in the square holes, and airy fabric curtains. Colorful wall tapestries and paintings appeared, as well as a vase of flowers on the table.

"It's not enough," I said. "Take more."

Suddenly, I saw a small, circular garden appear at the back of the house surrounded by a gray circular wall made of the same cement material as the house. It was connected to the house so that the only way into it was to walk through the house. Inside the garden, there was a fountain, a bench, grass, a little path, and flowers and trees everywhere.

Again, I saw a vision of what was to take place once my mother reached this house. There, I saw her little soul, sitting, uncertainly on the garden bench, Jesus beside her. I knew He was explaining to her all about what had happened in her life, where she was, and what was going to happen now. I knew it was significant that the garden was circular in shape like her cage had been and enclosed; she needed to feel something familiar in order to embark on this journey that Jesus was placing before her. I knew also that He was taking slow, small, gradual steps with her in her understanding and her trust. She looked unsure, but she looked up at Him and seemed to agree to trust Him to lead her on this journey.

Without asking I knew it was to be the journey of healing and growth that her soul had been denied in this lifetime. I knew also without being told that it would take at least as long as a full human lifetime to accomplish. The human soul is not a simple thing. It is complex and nuanced. It cannot be unraveled in an instant, even in heaven.

While her spirit lay recovering on a sick bed within the house, her soul remained in the garden, waiting. I saw Jesus return to her there day after day, speaking to her, helping her through whatever she could begin to understand at her stage of growth.

I turned back to the Holy Spirit. Remembering the dream my mother originally had for her life on earth, I asked, "Will Jesus teach her to dance?"

When I looked back at the house, I saw Jesus standing in the garden, my mother's little soul grasping His hands and standing on top of His feet. Jesus took the steps, and she was along for the ride as they circled joyfully around and around the circular path of the garden. She smiled and laughed. I suddenly saw a flash forward in time and my mother's soul now looked several years older. She had appeared about three years old previously, and now she looked between ten and twelve. She was still wearing a yellow dress, but now she danced on her own two feet in circles, still holding Jesus' hands. Her steps were confident, joyous, as if she knew the dance well. And I knew that one day, her soul would reach the same age as her spirit, her spirit would be well, and they would be reunited into a whole person.

"If she's still here when I arrive, may I come to see her?" I asked the Holy Spirit.

"Yes," She said simply.

I then saw myself some time after arriving in heaven. I was again dressed in full silver armor from head to toe, sword at my side. I walked directly into the house where my mother's spirit lay on the cot and knelt down beside her. I knew her sickness was from grief over the things she had done to others in her life. And I knew that she would need some help in her recovery.

As I knelt beside her, I grasped her hand. I felt compelled by the deepest compassion I have ever experienced to aid in her healing. Looking up at her I said, "I see you. I forgive you. I love you. I thank you. I honor you. You are not forgotten." She gave me a weak smile, but I knew it was significant. Forgiveness was somehow essential for her spirit's recovery from this grief, and it brought new meaning to John 20:23: *"If you forgive anyone's sins, they are forgiven; if you do not forgive them, they are not forgiven."* It became clear to me that forgiveness is a family affair. If we remember that forgiveness is, essentially, the release of a wrong, when I forgive someone else, I am not only allowing my own healing and restoration. I am releasing them into theirs, breaking the hold within which the bondage of their own actions against me has trapped them.

I stood up and walked out to the garden. There was Jesus with my mother's soul, looking like the three-year-old as I had first seen her. I knelt in front of her and leaned over. She seemed to already know who I was. I kissed her gently on her forehead.

She looked up at me, eyes shining. "When I grow up, I want to be just like you," she said with a hope-filled expression.

"You will be," I said, though I knew I meant in wholeness and maturity, not in design. We are entirely different creatures.

I flashed forward again to a time yet further into the future of my mother's journey, when she had fully healed and reunited the parts of herself together. She was an adult now.

I stood in a crowd of observers in the throne room of heaven as a line of dancers in white dresses made their way gracefully into the room. They began to perform a beautiful, worshipful dance in front of the Father's throne. They were filled with joy, celebration, and life. My mother was there at the head of the line, dancing with all of her heart. She was again the delicate flower, the gentle woman of earlier times. And yet, she was more. The substance of her was more solid. She was really an adult now, older than she had been before going to the earth. Her dream had come true. She was a dancer. She would be forever able to live out the cry of her heart, the call of her spirit. The sorrow of her past was left behind—all of life before her.

I watched her and was overwhelmed with pride in my little sister. She had done it. She had come through the pain, the suffering. She had reached the end, which was just the beginning. I felt a sense of completion. My job here was done. She didn't need me anymore. I did not even necessarily feel that our relationship would be particularly close from this point forward. It had been based on a mission, after all, and the mission was over. But I knew there would always be a point of connection between us. We had been part of each other's childhoods, but had now grown toward our own paths not likely to converge often.

As I have typed this encounter out on my computer, there sits beside me on the table a pile of used tissues from the weeping I have done. Whenever I think I've stopped being impacted by this encounter, all I need to do is recount it and I weep like I've only just understood its meaning. This pile of tissues has been nearly equal in size with every subsequent editing of this chapter. I hope I never become immune to the truths that were planted in my soul from this experience.

If you have not guessed, I have forgiven my mother. Not only have I forgiven her, but I love her deeply, immovably. I do not expect to have a renewed relationship with her in this life. It would be, frankly, pointless. The true person is buried and caged, and I cannot reach her. But the hope I have for restoration in eternity is unlike anything I have experienced before or since.

Heaven can seem, at times, like some distant, unknown place of fairytale and mystery. It is filled with the mystery of the Creator, to be sure. But it is not distant. This life will be over in a breath, in a blink, and our real lives will begin once that graduation test has been completed. Things that cannot be restored here will be restored there.

I do not say this to encourage you to give up on your journey of growth and maturity here. Just the opposite. Whatever we do here, we do not have to do there, and remember that here is where we earn the treasures. Here is where we gain the authority required to reign with Christ on the new-made earth for eternity. Here is where we have the opportunity to suffer and give Him our worship in the midst of it. We will not have this opportunity there. But I say this to you because not every situation in this life is up to our choice.

If I could, I would choose for my mother to be healed instantly, now, and have the chance to fill up her house with treasures. As it is, I have thought a number of times about how I can convince my siblings to donate to the cause and give some of their treasures to her, but ultimately, the decision is not mine. She has free will, as does my father and every other human being on this earth. We can and should do everything within our power to mature, heal, and step into our calling and authority in this lifetime. But when we fail, or when others fail us, or another person's decision prevents us from attaining our desired goal, just know that once this life is over, your life has only just begun. He restores all things, renews all things. If it is not accomplished here, it is not lost.

CHAPTER 25

And the God of all grace, who called you to his eternal glory in Christ, after you have suffered a little while, will himself restore you and make you strong, firm and steadfast.

—1 Peter 5:10

After I had this encounter with the Holy Spirit, I was struck by the similarities of the things I had witnessed to the Catholic concept of purgatory. Now, make no mistake, what I saw taking place with my mother took place in heaven. It was not in some other location, some other realm. However, it was separated, or rather, secluded from what I would call the central part of heaven, which had seemed much more like an enormous city in the periphery of my vision than the wooded mountainscape of my mother's house of healing.

The idea that once we reach heaven we must still complete a process, one that may involve healing, growth, and its associated pain, that there may be things we have yet to accomplish after this life, could be theologically difficult for some to accept. I understand why. I have heard many a preacher claim that when we die and enter heaven, every tear will be wiped away, implying our sorrows instantaneously vanish upon heaven's threshold. I would like to point out, however, that this is entirely unbiblical. There is a verse in the Bible that makes the statement that every tear will be wiped away and death, mourning, and crying will be no more (Revelation 21:4). But this verse is speaking in reference to the time when the earth is once again made new and the reign of Christ permanently and unalterably established upon its surface. It is not referring to our temporary stay in heaven before it is reunited with the new-made earth.

You will not find a verse in the Bible that claims there is no sorrow in heaven, but be assured that sorrow is not the stuff from which heaven is made. So, sorrow cannot long remain in an unaltered state once it arrives at heaven's doorway. I do not believe it's possible for unredemptive sorrow to exist within heaven's borders. But since we know the process of healing and growth invariably involves certain types of pain, I am convinced that such redeemed pain is not only allowable within heaven's gates, but it is a beautiful part of what it has to offer us in the completion of the working out of the salvation of our souls.

What I have pondered since having this encounter with the Lord involving my mother is the fact that it appears to me as though the Catholics are onto something. However, I want to be clear: I have no reason to believe (and I do not) that people are required to make any sort of payment for the sins they committed in life once they have died before they are allowed entrance into heaven. We know clearly from Scripture that all payment for our sin has already been made by the sacrifice on the cross. That is not what I am referring to. But it seems clear to me after this encounter with the Holy Spirit, that no matter when or at what stage of life a person dies, they may still be required to accomplish a certain level of growth before they're able to fully participate in the joys of life in heaven. Certain joys have been reserved for the mature family of God—for those able to bear the weight of the glory that exists in His direct presence.

When I say that I flashed forward to see what would take place in the future of my mother's journey in heaven, it seems almost as if there was a regular passage of time in heaven. I believe the Bible reveals that time on earth is an entirely different construct than time in heaven (2 Peter 3:8), and yet, there are things that take place in a sequenced order, it appears. God Himself exists outside of time, of course, but we are not God, and it seems clear that He created us with cumulatively progressing paths to walk. I do not claim to fully understand how this system operates once we are in heaven, but it is clear to me that the human soul requires the same space or "time" to process, heal, and mature, whether here or in heaven. God can and does accelerate the healing process for many, especially, I have found, for those who ask Him. But that simply means stuffing the same volume of healing and growth into a much shorter span of time. I can assure you this is not an "easier" path simply because it's shorter. It is, frankly, exhausting. But one thing is clear, the process must be completed in full. However we can conceptualize this, through the lens of time, or through the lens of process, the salient point is that it must be done completely and in a certain ordered sequence.

I have heard from mature believers from whose experiences I have greatly benefitted state that they believe it likely that children who die on this earth finish their growth into adulthood once they reach heaven. I would like to suggest that those who do not fully accomplish the growth and maturity of their soul here on the earth despite having reached physical adulthood will also still need to complete it once they have reached heaven in order to have the full privileges of spiritual adulthood in the Kingdom. It makes some sense. There are a great many privileges in our societies that are reserved for those who have reached the age of majority—the age considered to be a legal adult. We do not and should not allow children to make legally binding decisions, own property, get married, hold jobs, and a host of other activities that we recognize require some amount of experience and maturity to navigate. In many cases, these adult activities would be potentially harmful to the children themselves if they were allowed to participate in them.

The fact that the maturity of our souls is not based purely on time (as in the case of our physical bodies) does not negate the fact that we must reach a certain level of growth before we're able to adequately carry many of the spiritual assignments and activities the Lord wants to share with us. The maturing of our souls cannot be escaped. And it is clear to me that the maturation of our souls is not an instantaneous process here on the earth nor in heaven. It must be worked out. It does not rely on time, no. But it does require an exercise of our free will to pursue. We are simply too complex of beings to do it quickly and cheaply.

And this is a good thing. God designed us to be complex so that he can relate to us as true members of His family, rather than as simple creatures like our pets. Our faithful and loving dogs, to whom we relate on some level, could never share our dreams and hopes with any expectation of equal reciprocity. We are meant to be complex in order to relate to a complex God. And because of this, the working out of the maturity of our souls cannot be done in a moment, even if that moment is in heaven. It is unlikely that any human will have reached a state of perfect maturity—no more growth needed—before their life on this earth has ended. In fact, I don't believe it to be possible. But I also suspect that for some who reach heaven, the completion of their maturity will be a quick and simple process. Whereas, others like my mother will require a much greater level of process to reach completion. It also seems clear to me that this is entirely dependent upon the depths and lengths to which the individual was willing to go (or not) in this life to allow God to transform them into the healed, whole, mature being He designed them to be. If there are places in our lives, in our souls, that we are unwilling to examine, if there are places to which we are willing to say to God, "You may come here, but no further," then I believe we will find ourselves in this second category of people. This means we will be required to complete a significant segment of our journey of maturation in heaven, where we will not have the opportunity to earn treasures for our progress, where we will not be afforded the benefit of greater authority in the coming Kingdom for our efforts. Make no mistake, it will still be meaningful and important to complete the process. It will allow us to step into our majority, our adult spiritual inheritance, but it will not carry with it the same benefits as it would have if accomplished here and now.

I have come to believe that when the Bible speaks about the Bride of Christ making herself ready for His return (Revelation 19:7), the bride being ready is a prerequisite to His return. And I strongly suspect that what Jesus is waiting on in this hour is a bride who has reached maturity. We, as the church, can no longer afford to live out our lives in the escapist attitude: simply holding on inside our bubble until we "make it to heaven." We must mature beyond this. We must not put off our growth into adulthood until we have arrived in heaven. The time is coming when the remnant will be divided from the remainder of the church, which will not ultimately remain faithful to the Lord. The wheat will be divided from the tares and the sheep from the goats. And I do not believe this applies only to the church and the world. I believe it applies equally to within the church. When the enemy planted weeds in the wheat field (Matt. 13:24–43), he did so in the very same field. Why? So harvesters could not distinguish between the two *until they had reached maturity,* at which point, the weeds were separated from the wheat and burned.

The church is rapidly reaching a crisis point where a line will be drawn between the bride who is ready and the remainder of the church. Some will refuse to become the new wineskin. A line is drawn between the virgins who watch with a full supply of oil, prepared and ready, and those who are excluded from the marriage supper because they were unprepared. I believe one facet of this line is drawn between those who have been willing to face the brokenness, sin, wounds, and darkness resident within themselves and allow themselves to be utterly transformed by the healing and power of their Creator in order to reach maturity and those who have not. We can no longer afford to remain immature, hiding from our own dysfunction, selfishness, and unhealed pain. We must invite the Lord to examine and make known to us every corner of our souls where bondage, oppression, weakness, or wounding hides. We must invite Him to expose it to the light, for it will be brought out one way or another (Luke 12:2–3). Will we allow it to be brought out unto our maturity or unto our judgment?

I believe there are many currently within the church who believe themselves to be mature, but they are not. Their unwillingness to perform self-examination is a symptom of this immaturity and a cause of its continuation. I believe there are many within the church right now who believe themselves to be wheat, but they are tares, and they will find themselves excluded from the harvest. We are rapidly reaching the end of casual Christianity, and I, for one, thank God for this. The church has spent far too many decades, centuries, attending services, saying prayers, being sure not to drink heavily or use curse words, believing that good habits are the sum total of the Christian life on this earth. If we are *really* spiritual, we may even invite a coworker to church now and again.

In Matthew 24:24, we are told of a future time of great deception;

even the elect will be deceived, if that were possible, before Christ's return. What if the dividing line between the possibility and impossibility of the deception of the elect is their level of maturity and healing? After all, we have already understood that the great deception of Adam and Eve was the result of their immaturity. The great deception of the end-times world will not bypass believers simply because they happen to attend church and read their Bibles. After all, it did not bypass two people who met with God face-to-face daily in Eden. No, I believe we will need a much firmer foundation than going through the motions of Christianity, even firmer than genuinely held belief. We will need maturity, which, we have seen, only arises from experiences of suffering that we have allowed God to use as a tool of transformation within our souls.

It is time to set down the spirit of religion and all of our preconceived notions about what God will and won't do. Our beliefs about how God works are usually based on our own experiences. Instead, we should base our beliefs about our experiences on who God actually is. Church, it is time to relinquish control, self-righteousness, and judgment. It is time for those who claim to be the body of Christ to make themselves ready. If we are a body, then we are currently a sick body at best. We must become healthy. We must become mature. We must become those to whom the world feels confident in turning when overwhelmed by their own sickness and brokenness, not because of our gifts, but because of our health. This will not happen if what we have to offer them is more of the same with a different label attached. This will not happen if we leave our growth until we have reached heaven. We were given this life in which to mature, to heal, to become prepared to enter the active army of the living God.

Imagine the state of things on the earth if the entirety of the body of Christ had reached spiritual adulthood, while simultaneously, those who had gone to heaven before us completed their own journeys of maturity. We would be an army prepared for war, prepared for a final defeat of the powers of darkness. You see, our growth, healing, and maturity do not only affect us. They directly impact the level of readiness of the army of heaven for the ultimate destruction of darkness. And this also directly affects the timing of that destruction. I do not believe Yahweh will initiate the battle of the final annihilation of evil with an army of children at His back. No. He is waiting for them to graduate, to have been tested and found ready.

I say this not as someone who has reached full maturity, but rather, as someone who has recognized the desperate need for it.

Church, it is time. We must grow up. The process is hard, but it is good.

OVERVIEW OF THE HEALING PROCESS

My original intent for this book was not to include a detailed breakdown of the healing process itself, since my focus was the understanding of human suffering. However, it was suggested to me by several people that this might be a helpful section to include, so here is a brief overview of what I have learned about the healing process.

If we think of the soul's healing as a cake, there are various components, or "ingredients," that must be in the recipe. There are probably additional ingredients beyond those covered here that would make an even more complete cake, but these are the ones of which I have had the greatest revelations and experiences.

Understanding

Get wisdom; get understanding; do not forget, nor turn away from the words of my mouth.

—Proverbs 4:5

I will begin by discussing one of the most important ingredients of my own healing: understanding. Nearly every time I have found myself in need of healing, I have also found myself confused over the causes of my dysfunction and how to heal from it. This is understandable because we really only know what we have been taught in our families of origin and through life experiences. Mine taught me much about how to operate in dysfunction but not much about healthy functioning. Here are a few examples.

I knew I was extremely susceptible to being influenced by controlling and abusive partners. Still, I couldn't grasp the cure for this susceptibility without fully understanding what had brought me to it. When I began to delve into deeper research on the topic of narcissistic abuse, I began to recognize my parents in nearly every description of narcissistic behavior I came across. I gathered as much information as possible to understand its effect on human emotional and psychological development. This led me to discover that my parents' abusive behaviors had primed my brain to accept abuse and neglect as normal parts of life. It had also created in me a set of traits that not only allowed abusers to take advantage of me but drew them to me like moths to a flame. It also drew me to them, as my brain only knew how to "successfully" function in one type of environment: abusive.

Armed with this knowledge, I began to unlearn everything my parents had taught me to believe about myself. I sought out books, podcasts, and other resources for specific guidance on deprogramming the co-dependent brain and healing from narcissistic abuse.

Another example of how understanding played a vital role in my healing journey is when I had to face my feelings and beliefs about men. I wish I could state this in a less volatile way, but that would be dishonest. I hated men—hated them from the depths of my soul and with every fiber of my being. I saw them as weak, controlling toddlers in adult bodies, and the only reason to keep them around was the procreation of the species. I had a clear sense of why I felt this way. My father had failed to protect me in every conceivable way. I had endured very abusive relationships with men and did not have one man in my life who could help me extract myself from those relationships. A complete stranger even assaulted me in a public place, and the police officers to whom I reported the assault (all men) did absolutely nothing to bring me justice. The perpetrator faced no legal consequences for his actions. These are just a few of the many examples of what I saw as the failures of men in my life.

My experiences with men in the church had taught me that they were the worst of all because they pretended to be something they were not: honorable and good. In fact, church men demonstrated they were usually much worse when it came to control and oppression of women than men in the world, usually having deeper issues with predatory, manipulative, and addictive behaviors than the non-believing men I encountered. I vowed to never date or marry a Christian (even though I was one). I had not had contact with men who possessed anything resembling honor in the church.

But for some time, I was not concerned about the beliefs I held about men. They were not simply subconscious, underlying beliefs that needed to be exposed to be dealt with. I believed these things consciously and in full awareness. I had no problem voicing my opinions about the male species when needed. And I felt fully justified in my opinion. My need in this situation was not to understand *why* I felt the way I did. I knew why. It was to understand that my belief was an inaccurate and incomplete picture of reality.

As I embarked on my healing journey, I realized my perception of men was not in line with God's heart, but it seemed to me that His image in men had been lost somewhere along the way. I didn't even *want* to see them differently, but I began to ask Him to give me at least some desire to forgive or have compassion on men. Then, a realization came: I didn't need to understand why I felt the way I did about men, what I need to know was why the ones I had encountered had acted the way they did. I didn't need to understand me; I needed to understand them.

So, I began the search for resources to help me understand. I am sad to say it was difficult to find Christian resources about men that didn't just prop up old stereotypes and cliches about men being "less emotional" than women and needing to be "strong" all the time. I knew those ideas were insufficient. They were the tropes in which all the controlling men in my childhood church had been brought up. I was relieved to finally come across resources from people like Jason Vallotton and John Eldredge, who offered significantly better insights into how God had designed men and why this design has so often seemed to be distorted in my experiences with them. Without this understanding, I would never have been able to take the subsequent steps I needed to forgive and develop compassion for the millions of men around the world who truly are lost and can't seem to find their way back to the manhood God designed them for without help.

Understanding, in my opinion, is one of the most foundational steps to any journey of healing. For me, it was often the catalyst for taking the more difficult steps of forgiving and healing from any particular wound.

"And you will know the truth, and the truth will set you free" (John 8:32) has been a life verse of mine regarding healing. I have found that I cannot approach any situation where healing is required without first gaining an understanding of what I am being healed from and at least some measure of understanding of what my responsibility will be in the process. The truth has not always been pleasant. It has not always been what I wanted to know, but it has always brought me to new levels of freedom.

Revelation

However, as it is written:
"What no eye has seen, what no ear has heard, and what no human mind has conceived"—the things God has prepared for those who love him—these are the things God has revealed to us by his Spirit.
The Spirit searches all things, even the deep things of God.

—1 Corinthians 2:9–10

Following on the heels of understanding is a second essential component of healing: revelation. Understanding is a great first step, but it's just the start. Much of therapy and counseling involves helping people understand things they have experienced and the effects those experiences have had on them. This often extends to learning skills to retrain the human mind into new ways of thinking and approaching the world. This approach to inner healing is an important piece in the overall picture. It is needed, but it is not the end.

There is a step beyond natural, physical, human capacity that I believe is necessary to complete healing. It must involve God speaking directly to His children. The lies we learn about ourselves and our experiences most often come from the people closest to us. The truth must come from an even deeper, even truer source. For example, my human father led me to believe I was a mostly incompetent and intellectually inferior waste of space. His highest hopes for me appeared to be that he could marry me off young to someone of his choosing and make me someone else's problem. My Heavenly Father, however, has shown me time and time again that He trusts me with difficult assignments, situations that require wisdom and insight, and above all, that He loves me for my heart more than for anything I could achieve.

The revelations I detailed earlier in this book, which the Holy Spirit and the Father gave me regarding my parents, changed the course of my life. I knew a lot about my mother's family and her history. I had every reason to feel good, "Christian" compassion for her, but it remained an abstract concept in my head. Likewise, I understood my father's past and the trauma he had suffered. I could clearly see what led him to behave the way he had toward my siblings and me. Intellectually I knew God loved him. But it was not until God gave me a revelation of what his own heart felt toward my father and toward my mother when the abstract, psychological understanding I had gained finally permeated the barrier between my brain and my heart. It was not until that time that my soul was able to engage with the truth.

You see, God gave humans intelligence, insight, creativity, and the capacity to work out difficult problems. He gave us the ability to discover the many tools of healing available to us through psychology, therapy, and human relationships. There is, however, a level of healing that can only be found when the Creator of the universe, and your very soul, tells you who you are and shows you how He sees things. When He opens both your mind and your heart to see things as they truly stand, we see past our limited human perspective, warped by pain and suffering. Through His eyes, we stand outside the boundaries of time and the chains of trauma, so when He gives you a glimpse of the clarity with which He views your life, you cannot help but be transformed. His ways are not our ways, and His thoughts are not our thoughts (Isaiah 55:8). When we come into contact with His thoughts, our own seem suddenly to be thin, pale things that would be better tossed in the trash bin than hanging around in our heads. They don't even make much sense after you've heard what God has to say about your situation.

It would be difficult for me to count the number of times I have been wallowing in the depths of despair one moment and laughing at my own idiocy and immaturity the next. And what sparked this change? He spoke to me. What a good God who says that if we seek Him with all of our heart, He will be found by us (Jeremiah 29:13). What a good God who allows us access to His thoughts and feelings when we seek Him, who tells us the truths that will permanently alter us if we ask Him.

Internalization

When your words came, I ate them; they were my joy and my heart's delight, for I bear your name, LORD God Almighty.

—Jeremiah 15:16

Internalization is the step that must come after revelation. It is the process by which we take what God has shown us and make it our own. God showed me the love He felt for my father. I chose to agree with His assessment and take that love on as my own. Since then, I have never viewed my father in the same light nor felt toward him the same feelings I did previously. I can say the same about my mother.

It can be a quick process when your heart is set on God. I accepted the things God showed me about my parents and almost instantly took on His perspective of them as my own. Sometimes it may require a bit more struggle. Sometimes we don't really want to let someone "off the hook," so to speak, and so we feel resistant to what God has revealed to us as truth. Sometimes we like our anger, and we feel we have a right to it. But I can assure you that God's perspective is always the right one, and the sooner we align our own hearts and minds with His, the sooner we will reach our own freedom.

Verses

Hosea 4:6: "My people are destroyed for lack of knowledge."

Ephesians 1:17: "I keep asking that the God of our Lord Jesus Christ, the glorious Father, may give you the spirit of wisdom and revelation in the knowledge of him."

Proverbs 4:5–9: "Get wisdom, get understanding; do not forget my words or turn away from them. Do not forsake wisdom, and she will protect you; love her, and she will watch over you. The beginning of wisdom is this: Get wisdom. Though it cost all you have, get understanding. Cherish her, and she will exalt you; embrace her, and she will honor you. She will give you a garland to grace your head and present you with a glorious crown."

Proverbs 3:13: "Blessed is the one who finds wisdom, and the one who gets understanding."

Activity

Isaiah 11 says about Jesus, "The Spirit of the Lord will rest on him—the Spirit of wisdom and of understanding, the Spirit of counsel and of might, the Spirit of the knowledge and fear of the Lord."

If the Messiah Himself needed the Spirit of wisdom, understanding, counsel, might, and knowledge while He was on the earth to fulfill His calling, how much more do we?

1: Invite the Spirit of wisdom, knowledge, understanding, counsel, and might to have full access to your mind and heart. Tell the Lord you are willing to know the truth no matter what that truth looks like, and ask Him to reveal it to you in His perfect timing.

2: Research some areas of dysfunction you have noticed in your internal world (mind/heart) or your external world (behaviors/reactions). It can be as simple as typing into your search bar, "Why do I ___ when ___ happens?" If you find some interesting information, read or listen to more sources on the topic.

Forgiveness

Do not repay evil with evil or insult with insult. On the contrary, repay evil with blessing, because to this you were called so that you may inherit a blessing.

—1 Peter 3:9

I wrote earlier about forgiveness and its importance, so this will not be a long section. I would like to reiterate a few things here, namely how forgiveness cannot be accomplished until we have been willing to feel the depths of the pain caused to us by those we need to forgive. Also, voice must be given to the real and actual harm (and sometimes even the imagined or perceived harm) that was caused to us by them. Do not bother trying to forgive without first going through this step. It cannot work. This step can take some time, depending on the depth of the pain. I have spent the better part of a year focused on forgiving one person, even while fully open to my own emotions and the pain they had caused me. In a state of complete willingness and desire to forgive, the pain still often comes in waves. It is frequently healed by peeling off one layer of hurt at a time, and as we are mere human beings, we many times cannot withstand the level of pain we would experience were we to feel it all at once. So, be willing to feel it all, even in pieces, and be willing to make some commitment of time to the process. Have patience. If it is in your heart to forgive and you are seeking God in every step, it will work in the end.

Secondly, remember that forgiveness is, at its core, the simple act of letting go. You will know forgiveness has taken root when you no longer feel the need for that person (or for other people) to know you were right, to know you were the wronged party. When you no longer have something to prove, when you no longer feel that they owe you something. You will know forgiveness has taken root when you can feel pain in your heart *for* them instead of *from* them, knowing their actions may result in their own harm, not just yours.

As a final note on forgiveness, it is essential to living life as a believer that we learn to view people from God's perspective rather than our own. If you are struggling to forgive someone, ask God to show you how He sees them. He may not show you in a way you expect, but He does not withhold good things from those who walk in righteousness (Psalm 84:11), and His perspective is a good thing.

Verses

Matthew 18:21–22: "Then Peter came to Him and said, 'Lord, how often shall my brother sin against me, and I forgive him? Up to seven times?' Jesus said to him, 'I do not say to you, up to seven times, but up to seventy times seven.'"

Matthew 6:14–15: "For if you forgive other people when they sin against you, your heavenly Father will also forgive you. But if you do not forgive others their sins, your Father will not forgive your sins."

Activity

Ask the Lord, "Who do I need to forgive?" and "What experiences do I need to forgive for?" Let the Holy Spirit show you places in your soul, maybe some long-forgotten, where you have harbored unforgiveness. Remember, don't be afraid of what the Holy Spirit might reveal to you. The truth will set you free, and allowing yourself to feel the pain of those memories is the first step toward true forgiveness.

Will/Choice

But if serving the Lord seems undesirable to you, then choose for yourselves this day whom you will serve, whether the gods your ancestors served beyond the Euphrates, or the gods of the Amorites, in whose land you are living. But as for me and my household, we will serve the Lord.

—Joshua 24:15

Another vital component of the healing process is that of *will*. I do not mean willpower, which is the attempt to accomplish something in your own strength. What I mean is your *choice*. God gave us free will to choose Him or to choose other things—other means by which to attempt to make ourselves feel full. If we would like, we have every right to remain in our broken, damaged state, harming others around us, and unable to accomplish the things we were made to do. It's a painful way to live, but if you'd rather have that pain than the pain of healing, you are allowed to keep it.

Likewise, healing cannot begin unless you choose it as what you want and what you will pursue. You may not have the strength to actually accomplish it. That's not an abnormal condition. In fact, it is a human condition. But the point is, you choose it. God honors your free will so much that if you make the choice to pursue healing, He will meet you in places where you have no ability to effect change on your own; He will bring with Him the very tools and people you need to take your next step.

The most significant part of using your will to choose is that you agree to submit your will to His. You choose to want what He wants, even if it's painful, difficult, time-consuming, and exhausting. You must give Him your *yes* without strings attached, without a place where you tell Him He can't go any further.

Sometimes you will find yourself in a place where you lack the ability to choose His way. It is beyond your capacity. That's okay. He's fine with that. In fact, this is usually where the greatest changes take place. As long as the desire of your heart is to want what He wants (even if you don't currently want it, but you want to want it), as long as you tell Him "yes," even when you don't have the capacity to act on that yes, it is all He needs to work miracles in your soul and in your life. Philippians 2:13 says, "for it is God who works in you to will and to act in order to fulfill his good purpose." It isn't up to you alone. The more you choose Him in your heart, regardless of your ability to act on that choice, the more you give God space to work in you to strengthen and redeem your will. If God has your unconditional *yes*, there is nothing He cannot do inside you. I dare you to test Him.

Verses

Romans 12:2: "Do not conform to the pattern of this world, but be transformed by the renewing of your mind. Then you will be able to test and approve what God's will is—his good, pleasing and perfect will."

John 5:19: "Jesus gave them this answer: 'Very truly I tell you, the Son can do nothing by himself; he can do only what he sees his Father doing, because whatever the Father does the Son also does.'"

As Christians, our goal is to become more like Christ all the time. If Jesus' will was so aligned with and submitted to the Father's will that He only did what He saw the Father doing, this should be our ultimate goal as well.

Activity

1: In order to align our will with God's, we must allow our minds to be renewed. Invite the Lord to have access to your mind to begin the process of renewal so your thoughts begin to look like His thoughts. The renewal of your mind is an essential step on the path to the transformation of your will.

2. Identify one area in your life where your will (choices) are not aligned with God's heart or His design for you. Tell the Lord that you choose in your heart His ways instead of your own and ask Him to meet

you in this choice. This could be an addictive coping mechanism (anything from drugs, to pornography, to a sugar addiction), which is really just anything you consistently turn to for comfort instead of the Lord. Tell the Lord (if you mean it in your heart) that you choose to submit your will to His. Tell Him you want what He wants, or at the very least, you *want to want it*.

3. Research some resources online or in your local area that offer counseling services for things like addiction, unhealthy coping mechanisms, and long-term effects of relational trauma, and make an appointment to engage with one of these resources.

Time

He has made everything beautiful in its time. He has also set eternity in the human heart; yet no one can fathom what God has done from beginning to end.

—Ecclesiastes 3:11

One of the most frustrating pieces of the healing puzzle for me has been time. I am someone who loves to check things off my to-do list. There are few things more satisfying in this life, in my opinion. If they need doing, I want them done.

Unfortunately, healing is one of the most time-consuming, process-based activities I have ever been involved in. You cannot heal a soul overnight any more than you can grow a tree in the same span of time. Growth is slow. It takes time. It takes care and intentional effort. Some seasons will be a lot faster and more densely packed with growth than others, but they still will all require time.

Why is this? Well, we are complex creatures. Like onions (and Shrek), people have layers, and each one must be dealt with in its season. If God were to cut open the entire soul of a human at once and have us feel, grieve, understand, and process every wound we'd ever received simultaneously, I don't think many of us would survive the wreckage. I certainly would not. I am thankful that God didn't let me see at the outset how long my healing journey would take. I probably would not have embarked on it if I had known because it would have felt utterly overwhelming and impossible. However, choosing to pursue the healing of my soul has proven to be the best decision (and decision, and decision, and decision, day after day, after day) I have ever made.

It is tempting to feel frustrated at times with the slowness of the progression of healing. It often feels like plodding along one heavy step at a time and barely getting anywhere. However, you do reach a point where you can look back and say, "I feel like I've made no progress at all, yet I am miles away from where I started. I do not even recognize that person anymore."

It is also tempting to give up in the middle. You wonder how you can bear any more of the weight of examining and feeling your pain and suffering while seeming to go nowhere. Many verses in the Bible implore us to persevere in the face of difficulty, trial, and suffering. Paul tells us the rewards of keeping the faith until the end, "finishing the race" (2 Timothy 4:2– 8). Inner healing, which is really the sanctification of our souls, does not in recent decades seem to have been taught broadly as a vital component of our faith, but the Bible, the early church fathers, and the whole of Christianity for centuries disagree with that notion. If we are to endure, persevere, and keep our faith to the end, a large part of endurance involves not giving up on the process of the healing of our souls. It is my strong belief that God intends for us to use this life to become both whole and mature. We will not accomplish this if we give up somewhere in the middle because it got difficult or took too long.

Certainly, there are moments when you will need some respite. You will need a break, a time to recover from the often painful process of growth and healing. Just don't allow yourself to remain there permanently. God has too many amazing things for you to experience and do in this life to miss out because you gave up on your healing.

As Winston Churchill is attributed with saying, "If you're going through hell, keep going." You never know when life-changing breakthrough is only the next step away.

Verses

Galatians 5:22–23: "But the fruit of the Spirit is love, joy, peace, **patience**, kindness, goodness, faithfulness, 23 gentleness, self-control; against such things there is no law."

Hebrews 12:1–2: "Therefore, since we are surrounded by such a great cloud of witnesses, let us throw off everything that hinders and the sin that so easily entangles. *And let us run with perseverance the race marked out for us*, fixing our eyes on Jesus, the pioneer and perfecter of faith. For the joy set before him he endured the cross, scorning its shame, and sat down at the right hand of the throne of God."

Ecclesiastes 3:1: "There is a time for everything, and a season for every activity under the heavens."

Activity

1: There will be times when the healing process frustrates you and feels like it is moving at a snail's pace. Ask God to help you understand the times and seasons in your life so you can know what part of your healing He wants you to focus on in each season. Ask Him also to help you gain patience to be content with your journey and progress at His pace.

2: The Serenity Prayer, often used in addiction recovery programs, can be helpful with gaining patience for God's timing.

"God grant me the serenity to accept the things I cannot change; courage to change the things I can; and wisdom to know the difference."

Grace

And God is able to make all grace abound to you, so that having all sufficiency in all things at all times, you may abound in every good work.

—2 Corinthians 9:8

I am what you might call a *doer*. The moment I realize something needs to be done, I start planning a strategy and taking steps to make it happen. I don't know why exactly (I suspect some connection to my autistic brain), but if I know something needs to be fixed or changed, I cannot relax until it has been. I have often found myself frustrated with the fact that God tends not to tell me what the next step is until it is time to take it. I suspect this is because He knows I would take it immediately when He might want me to wait a bit.

Because of this drive, I embarked on my healing journey with that same mentality. I would find every crack and damaged corner of my soul and systematically eliminate them until there were none left. It was a good plan. It has helped me much along the way. But it left very little room for God's grace in the planning. I intended to attack brokenness with every bit of strength and mental fortitude I could muster. Unfortunately, it took me quite a while down this path to realize that I was often relying on my own strength, willpower, and drive to accomplish this task. I've never found it easy to reach the end of myself and realize there's nothing more I can do. But I have reached it many times on this trek toward wholeness.

Whether it is has been a pattern of thought, an addictive coping mechanism, or a specific habit or behavior, almost without exception I have fought against it with every fiber of my being only to come to a point where I have no more fight left. At this point, I have to say, "I want to do better at this, God, but I can't. You're going to have to do it." And He does.

The first time I handed it over to Him, it was a shock. I had long struggled with a tendency to fantasize about the future, imagining things turning out some specific way that would magically fix all my problems. I recognized it as an unhealthy coping mechanism, a type of escapism, and used every drop of willpower I had to stop those thoughts in their tracks. But I was so easily triggered into this coping mechanism by life's hardships, relationship difficulties, and negative experiences that it felt nearly impossible to stay on top of it all the time. I knew I ultimately needed many facets of my life and relationships to change in order for me to no longer feel that I needed that coping mechanism, but in the meantime, I was exhausted. I didn't have the energy to fight it off nearly as often as it cropped up.

Finally, worn out, I lay on my couch and cried.

"I'm sorry," I told God. "I tried. I don't know what else to do. You're going to have to do something."

I don't think I actually expected Him to. It was really just my way of telling Him *I give up*. However, I woke up the next day and was shocked to realize that the compulsion I'd been spending all my energy fighting was barely a factor. It was there. There were underlying needs and wounds that still needed addressing, but it had lost its teeth, its power. It just wasn't that hard to tell myself, "I don't need that anymore. Reality is actually better." And I meant it. Even though my reality was still not as God intended for me permanently, the fact that I had gained any freedom at all and that I had His presence constantly with me was better than any fake future I could invent for myself.

I can't say I never have moments when I still struggle with this temptation, but I can say there has always been improvement over time, not regression, and this has happened for me in many areas of struggle in my life. When I finally reach the end of my capacity, His grace is finally able to pick up the banner and fight on my behalf. I sometimes wonder, *how much more quickly my path toward wholeness would have gone if I had just stopped trying to do it all myself and let Him take care of it sooner?* And I've discovered in the process that I like the end of myself. It's a place without pressure and where there is nowhere else to go but up. I'm thankful to have found it.

Verses

Exodus 14:14: "The Lord will fight for you; you need only to be still."

Isaiah 41:10: "So do not fear, for I am with you; do not be dismayed, for I am your God. I will strengthen you and help you; I will uphold you with my righteous right hand."

Zechariah 4:6: "'Not by might nor by power, but by my Spirit,' says the Lord Almighty."

Activity

1: Ask the Lord to help you learn to know the difference between striving in your own strength and willpower and allowing His grace to hold you up in your struggles as you climb toward freedom and wholeness.

Community

Carry each other's burdens, and in this way you will fulfill the law of Christ.

—Galatians 6:2

The topic of community in the healing process has been an odd one for me. Having spent most of my life alone amongst crowds, I was used to doing everything myself. If there was a problem, it rarely crossed my mind to seek another person for assistance (it still frequently does not). When it did, I would rid myself of the thought instantly. I was convinced of what my mother had hammered into my head. If I asked for help or had any needs, people would dislike me and think I was using them or bothering them. As such, I embarked on my path to healing largely alone.

I spend hours every day reading, listening, journaling, watching… alone. I absorbed every small speck of information I could find on inner healing, theology, and psychological conditions. This time spent as a veritable sponge was irreplaceable to my healing process—absolutely necessary. However, I was under the fallacious impression that it was the full picture of the healing process. I had done everything else on my own, and this was how I intended to heal as well. And I will tell you that my capacity for solo achievement had always been high. If there was one person I would have expected to be able to tackle the difficult journey of healing on their own, it would have been me.

I could not.

I began to realize after a short time that, even though there were many areas of inner healing I could work on with only God and me, there were also many others that required additional human beings to be part of the equation. I began to understand that since humans were the ones who had primarily caused the damage in my soul, it could not be retrained or healed absent their presence. The deprivation of stable, loving, healthy family had been my soul's downfall. Its presence must necessarily be a component of my soul's resurrection.

As someone who has always prided myself on facing my fears head-on, I am a little embarrassed to admit how long it took me after having this revelation to actually reach out to real human beings for help. When I did, I started with total strangers who had no "skin in the game," so to speak. I went through several Sozo sessions through ministries like Bethel and similar types of inner healing experiences with other ministries. These were very helpful and I would strongly recommend them to anyone on their healing journey. They did, however, allow me the comfort of not having to speak to anyone I personally knew about the ugly things in my soul and risk losing the person's regard or relationship. They didn't know me. If they found me too needy, or my issues too difficult and burdensome, it wouldn't matter. I could easily cut them loose and move on.

This, I was to find, however, was not a great long-term healing strategy. What I needed were people who could walk with me on some kind of long-term basis, who could see the deep and dark and ugly and not be put off by it. This, I suspect, is a good definition of family.

I believe it took me longer to reach out to someone with whom I already had some connection than it had to reach out to a total stranger. It was well worth it in the end, however. The healing and growth I have gained from the small number of people who have seen the ugliest parts of me has launched me further into the health and wholeness of my soul than any other step I have taken.

There is no substitute for vulnerable, safe relationships with other people. God designed us to have them, and we will not and cannot function as He intended us to without them, which means that healing is not possible without them.

Besides good, healthy, encouraging friends, for many people it will be important to find a good therapist or counselor with whom they can meet regularly along the way. There are many times when what you really need is an impartial, objective perspective on the difficulties through which you are working. And while friends and family often love and want to help, their own emotional investment in you may cloud their ability to see things in your life clearly, or they may simply not have the requisite knowledge to help you through certain parts of your healing journey. Additionally, there have been moments in my own journey when I was so overwhelmed by the weight of what I was processing that I would likely have given up on the whole thing if I had not had a regularly scheduled appointment already on the calendar to look forward to for some guidance.

Verses

James 5:16: "Therefore, confess your sins to one another and pray for one another, that you may be healed. The prayer of a righteous person has great power as it is working."

Hebrews 10:24–25: "And let us consider how we may spur one another on toward love and good deeds, not giving up meeting together, as some are in the habit of doing, but encouraging one another—and all the more as you see the Day approaching."

Romans 12:4–5: "For just as each of us has one body with many members, and these members do not all have the same function, so in Christ we, though many, form one body, and each member belongs to all the others."

Activity

1: If you have healthy, loving believers in your life already, make a commitment to meet with them regularly to honestly and openly share your healing journey and receive prayer and feedback from them.

2: If you do not already have such people in your life, commit to researching church communities in your area or online with thriving inner-healing ministries and support groups. Choose one, and reach out to become connected with other believers who are chasing after the same goals as you.

3: If you have deep trauma in your past and have not yet begun to meet regularly with a therapist or counselor who works with trauma victims, research options available to you in your area or online to begin this journey with some objective input.

4: If you do not yet feel as though you've found it, ask the Lord to help you find your place in the body of believers, your tribe, your spiritual family, your community.

Deliverance

For we do not wrestle against flesh and blood, but against the rulers, against the authorities, against the cosmic powers over this present darkness, against the spiritual forces of evil in the heavenly places.

—Ephesians 6:12

A key ingredient in the healing cake will often be deliverance. The expulsion of demonic spirits has long been a controversial topic in Christianity. Can Christians even be demonized? Is there a difference between possession and oppression? How would we tell if we need deliverance from demonic spirits?

Whatever your theological persuasion on the topic, I can personally attest that yes, believers can, in fact, be demonized. The most common place for a demon to attach itself to a human being is an area of woundedness or unmet need in the soul or some lie that the soul has believed. They latch on and use the wound, lack, or incorrect belief to convince us of lies about ourselves, others, God, and the world around us, and to either suggest unhealthy coping mechanisms to our vulnerable, wounded minds, or to urge us on to greater depths of bondage in unhealthy coping mechanisms that we've already established. They will stay there, latched on, until we make them leave.

One way to recognize if a demonic spirit has attached itself to you is to take stock of your reactions to difficult situations. Often, there is an element of compulsion involved with demonization that manifests as feeling as though you have no choice in your own behavior, even if you recognize it as unhealthy and want it to change. This is, of course, a common element of emotional triggers and addictive behavior as well, but I would like to suggest that you would be hard pressed to find a person in full-blown addiction who does not also have a demonic spirit specifically connected to that addictive coping mechanism. If your primary means of receiving spiritual information is by feeling (or even potentially if it is not), you may feel a specific sensation directly associated with giving in to the compulsive or addictive behavior. Generally, you will have long perceived this to be a good feeling, which reinforces the unhealthy behavior.

I once knew a person who described their addiction to food in this way. When the person ate food as a way to feel in control or to cope with difficult emotions, they felt a rush go through their head and down through their body. Now, giving into addictions can certainly trigger a release of dopamine in the brain (that is often what perpetuates the addiction in a biological sense), but that is not something typically felt as a physical sensation like a rush of liquid going through the entire body. I recognized this description, having had my own similar experiences when giving in to my addictions. It is entirely demonic in nature and has generally been a factor in our lives for so long that we don't realize it is not just our own body's response or sensation, but an outside force intent on keeping us in bondage.

As you may imagine, the trauma I had experienced in my life left me with quite a few wounds and areas of lack to which demonic spirits could attach. It took me a number of years to determine which things I felt and thought were my own original experiences and which were the influence of demonic spirits. This was a long and arduous process, but well worth it. It has helped me to immediately recognize when one of these spirits tries to return and restart old patterns. It has, in fact, dramatically increased my ability to discern spirits.

In my experience, one of the surest ways to be rid of a demonic spirit is to heal the wounded or lacking place in your soul or the lie to which it has attached itself. It leaves no place for that demon to dock itself. However, the process of healing deep wounds takes time. It is rarely an immediate result, and sometimes there is deliverance needed along the way to even make it possible to take the next step in your healing journey. I strongly advise deliverance to help you on your way if you are already committed to healing and you're taking steps to do so. If you are not in the process of healing and not able to fill in the spaces occupied by that demon with the Holy Spirit once it's gone, then deliverance will do you little good; it may even make things worse, as demons tend to return to empty houses with many more of their friends (Matthew 12:43–45). But for someone already taking steps into healing, deliverance is usually a vital piece to the puzzle.

Some people have questions about self-deliverance vs. having another believer take you through deliverance. I have experienced both. Demons have fled while I was alone with the Lord and when a fellow believer commanded them to go. If you are new to deliverance, I would highly recommend seeking out someone who has experience in the process to guide you.

It will be important to keep in mind that getting free of demonic spirits and staying free of them are two separate things. Getting free can often be done relatively quickly. But make no mistake, a demonic spirit will most often attempt to reestablish its hold at the first opportunity. Maybe it's when you are emotionally triggered, experiencing loss or grief, going through a time of instability, or having relationship difficulties. I would strongly admonish you not to be discouraged when this happens. It is often part of the process of gaining true and lasting authority over that spirit, which becomes easier and easier the further along you go in the healing of the wound that left you open to that spirit in the first place. Do not give into the temptation to believe the lies that you will never be truly free, that there is no light at the end of the tunnel. One of the surest ways to let a demonic spirit in is by believing its lies, and you can be sure that any thought trying to convince you to be impressed with a demon or convinces you of your own powerlessness and hopelessness is a *big fat lie*.

As a final thought on deliverance, I think it is important to note that it is not often pretty. I have vomited, convulsed, screamed, and a host of other strange manifestations as a demonic spirit was leaving my body. This is normal. They don't like to go, and they like to make a show whenever they can. Don't bother being afraid of them or impressed by their tantrums. This only gives them power. I would also suggest setting aside any fear of what other people may think of you during the deliverance process. It is very likely to be weird. Oh well, there's no getting around it. The real question is, do you want your freedom enough to set aside what other people might think about the fact that you've had a demonic spirit or that your body is doing odd things? You will need to want it badly enough to actually attain freedom.

Verses

Matthew 6:13: "And lead us not into temptation, but deliver us from the evil one."

1 John 3:8: "The one who does what is sinful is of the devil, because the devil has been sinning from the beginning. **The reason the Son of God appeared was to destroy the devil's work..**"

Galatians 5:1: "It is for freedom that Christ has set us free. Stand firm, then, and do not let yourselves be burdened again by a yoke of slavery."

Activity

1: Pray: "Lord, I give You permission to come into my soul and disrupt the works of the evil one. I give You full access to every part of my soul that needs to come into the light and be freed."

2: Research and find a resource either in your area or online that offers deliverance ministry, and set up a time to meet with someone from their ministry team.

Open-mindedness

*For God does speak—now one way, now another—
though no one perceives it.*

—Job 33:14

The idea of being open-minded tends to trigger some in the Christian community to rampant panic. Fears of believing false doctrine or being deceived have long been a facet of Christian life, unfortunately. This has led various branches of Christianity to claim that they alone have deciphered all correct doctrine, and anyone who disagrees with them is either greatly deceived or possibly unsaved. Such arrogance seems to be a common feature of many denominations and individual churches, but it really has no place residing within any believer—certainly not any believer who is on the often "shocking" journey of inner healing. One thing I've learned through the healing of my soul is that I know very little, and that God will send me the answers I need from unexpected places more often than from expected ones.

If you desire to become whole, I can confidently say holding rigidly to previously held pet doctrines, church structures, or non-essential beliefs will hinder you. Am I suggesting that we throw out every basic belief of Christianity and start from scratch? No, I am not. I will never accept as truth anything that contradicts the Word of God, the message of salvation through Jesus Christ, or who I know God to be from my relationship with Him. What I will also not do is try to fit Him in a box with which I am comfortable. Every person on earth is created in the image and likeness of God, endowed with a piece of His heart, His mind, His creative genius. This means every person on earth is a potential source of learning, whether they have found Him yet or not.

I am sad to say that in the course of my healing journey, I found more helpful information for understanding the past experiences that shaped me from non-Christian and completely secular sources than from Christian ones. There are certainly good Christian resources for inner healing and growth. I have listed some at the end of this book. Sadly, however, Christianity for so long rejected the very idea of psychology as a science and the understanding of how God created the human soul to function. So, in many places the church is far behind the world when it comes to helping broken and traumatized people. This is changing, and I look forward to seeing more of it as time goes on. But there appears to still be in some Christian circles a hesitancy or an outright fear of listening to anything about human experience that does not come from a strictly Christian source.

In my opinion, if the church was functioning the way God designed and intended it to, it would be the first place people in the world would turn for answers to difficult problems. We would be known as the people who have the solutions. It is not that way now, but it is a good goal to set.

In the meantime, we must be aware that God will use whatever means necessary to reach us if we are truly seeking Him and pursuing healing, and we must be willing to hear it. I can confidently say I would not have reached the place of healing I have now without a great many non-Christian sources of information, ranging from books and podcasts to scientific studies and medical reports. God placed His own image in each person, and, as a result, it is a human trait to seek truth. Even those who have not yet found the Truth, are likely to find some truth along the way. They simply won't have the full context for understanding its significance.

The idea that God can and will only speak through believers who share our theology is both harmful and, in my opinion, unbiblical. Moses, after all, learned a great deal about effective leadership from his father-in-law, Jethro, who was not Jewish, and, many scholars agree, was not likely a follower of Yahweh (Exodus 18:17–27). There is some debate on Jethro's religious affiliations, but it is clear that he was not Jewish and did not come from the same spiritual background as Moses and the Israelites.

God sent a pagan king, Cyrus, as the man who would free Israel from captivity and finance the rebuilding of the temple in Jerusalem (story found in the book of Ezra). He worked through Cornelius, a Roman centurion in the New Testament, to do good works for the Jews and the Jewish synagogue before he ever learned about Jesus as the Messiah (Acts 10). There is no magic switch that turns on in a person the moment they are saved, causing them to suddenly seek truth. Seeking truth is a condition of being human, and I doubt many people would have come to salvation without it. Can we find the complete truth outside of God? Of course not. Are we likely to find pieces of it deposited in people He made to be like Him? Yes, we are.

I am, of course, not suggesting that we go down strange spiritual paths and be open to other religions, gods, or spirituality devoid of the Holy Spirit. We know these will *not* lead to truth, but to bondage. However, we are likely to find nuggets of truth in surprising places. And this brings me to my next ingredient in the cake of healing.

Discernment

But the wisdom from above is first pure, then peaceable, gentle, open to reason, full of mercy and good fruits, impartial and sincere.

—James 3:17

On any journey of healing, you will be required to use discernment and wisdom to discover the truth that God desires you to learn in each moment. I stated earlier how I found a great deal of help from a number of non-Christian sources in my healing journey. This is true. However, I did not approach these sources without parameters and standards of judgment. Here are some of those standards.

1. Does a statement or idea directly contradict Scripture?
2. Does it teach something in violation of the heart of God as displayed in Scripture?
3. Does it violate what I know of God's character from my personal experience with Him?
4. Does it seem to bear good fruit?

There are a number of statements made clearly and without room for argument in the Bible. There are, of course, the central doctrines of our faith, namely salvation through the sacrifice of Jesus on the cross and His resurrection—and through no other means. The divinity and humanity of Jesus, the Trinity, the inerrancy of Scripture. These are all things foundational to our faith. There are also many clearly stated commandments in the Bible. The Ten Commandments and the commandments of the New Covenant given by Jesus during His ministry on earth are both examples of clear biblical commandments. Any statement you come across that violates essential doctrine or biblical commandment is not to be adhered to. It is false, plainly and simply. This means you must have a solid understanding of your faith and biblical literacy, and if you don't, you will need to actively check every statement against the Bible to judge it.

There are also many examples in the Bible where we see God not necessarily giving a direct commandment, but simply showing or telling us who He is. For example, God makes it clear that He is the only God, there is no other. If a source instructs you to pray to or follow any other spiritual or natural being as a deity, this is clearly unbiblical. The Bible is clear that God is kind, forgiving, patient, loving, and He desires for us to be the same. If you find a source of information encouraging you to act in spite, seek revenge, or harm another person, this is clearly unbiblical. There are, of course, other examples that are a bit more subtle, a bit less clear.

For example, while reading a book for people attempting to heal from the effects of sexual trauma, the (non-Christian) author stated that masturbation was a part of normal, healthy, adult sexuality, as long the person masturbating was only thinking about their partner or spouse while doing so. There is no direct prohibition against masturbation in the Bible, so this type of statement could be more difficult to judge than other, more clearly stated commandments. However, I had come to understand prior to reading this book much of God's character and His intent and purposes for sex and marriage. I was convinced that since masturbation eliminates half of the intended equation of intimacy for which God originally designed sex, it was not aligned with His design for sexual activity. This was based on a thorough study of the Bible and how God handles the subjects of intimacy and covenant throughout Scripture in both sexual and non-sexual contexts. I was not convinced to believe otherwise simply because a person who had learned a great deal about recovery from sexual trauma, but who did not personally know God, said so. There was truth to be gleaned from the book, certainly, but it was not a complete picture of truth, and, at times, it attempted to fill in the gaps with things I knew to be false. This is not a judgment of the author or the book. I knew this person was not a believer when I decided to read the book. I did not expect this author to speak as one. This is where discernment and wisdom are needed. We must be able to recognize important truths from any source we encounter while simultaneously recognizing when to reject things that do not reflect God's heart or His ways.

As a final assessment tool, I try to judge an idea based on the fruit it bears in people's lives. If I find that an idea does not contradict the Bible or God's character, I will often try to judge whether that idea has shown itself to be helpful and bear *good* fruit in the lives of people who have adhered to it. A bad tree cannot bear good fruit and vice versa (Matthew 7:18). I will often watch videos or read posts online by people who have tried certain therapeutic methods or approaches to healing to determine if good fruit has been borne. If a large number of normal, average humans have found help from a specific approach or idea, or if there are truly compelling stories of changed lives, then I will generally give it a chance and continue learning and applying that approach. Even if I have trouble finding reviews of a specific method of healing, I will often be willing to try it and see what fruit it bears in my own life.

The temptation for many is to think that because a source was right about one thing, it must be right about *all* things, or, conversely, to believe that if a source was wrong about one thing, there is *nothing* of value to glean from it. That is not how human beings work. Authors, podcasters, pastors, psychologists, and therapists are all human beings. There are very few people I have listened to or whose work I have read with whom I agree on every point. However, without many of them, I would not be the person I am today. It is part of, not just the healing journey, but the human journey to develop the skills necessary to weigh and test information in light of Scripture and sound theology. We must be able to throw out the bath water but keep the baby.

These dual ingredients of open-mindedness and discernment/ wisdom must be used hand-in-hand. Neither one is to be used on its own, otherwise you will end up rejecting every source (even the ones

God is sending your way) or accepting every strange idea that comes along. If you do not feel confident in your ability to rightly judge a healing resource, don't be alarmed. God has given us the Holy Spirit for guidance, and other believers with more experience and wisdom than we have to help us on our journey. And, as is always the case with God, He is much more concerned with the position of your heart than whether or not you make mistakes as you go.

But rest assured, if the mistakes you make on your journey lead you to pain or suffering, you now know a path to healing. God never promised us a pain-free life, but He did promise that He would never leave us nor forsake us along the way (Deuteronomy 31:8).

Verses

1 Corinthians 13:9–12: "For we know in part and we prophesy in part, but when completeness comes, what is in part disappears. When I was a child, I talked like a child, I thought like a child, I reasoned like a child. When I became a man, I put the ways of childhood behind me. For now we see only a reflection as in a mirror; then we shall see face to face. Now I know in part; then I shall know fully, even as I am fully known."

Proverbs 11:14: "For lack of guidance a nation falls, but victory is won through many advisers."

Proverbs 15:22: "Plans fail for lack of counsel, but with many advisers they succeed."

1 Thessalonians 5:20–22: "Do not treat prophecies with contempt but test them all; hold on to what is good, reject every kind of evil."

1 John 4:1: "Dear friends, do not believe every spirit, but test the spirits to see whether they are from God, because many false prophets have gone out into the world."

Activity

1: Pray this prayer from Proverbs 119:125: "I am your servant; give me discernment that I may understand your statutes."

2: Pray: "Lord, send me the people and the resources I need to continue on this journey. Help me to lay aside any prejudices or preconceived ideas about where Your help may come from."

———

There are other ingredients in the healing cake I could discuss, such as gratitude and humility. However, I feel like these things are largely encompassed in the components I have already listed. Forgiveness, for example, requires humility, as does open-mindedness. The pieces I have discussed here are absolutely essential for successful healing. God may highlight others or some of these more than others to you on your own path to healing, so don't feel that your journey must look like a specific outline of this list. Each person is uniquely individual, and God will meet you in the places where you need Him the most.

I hope this list has been helpful to you as a starting point toward wholeness.

For this reason, since the day we heard about you, we have not stopped praying for you. We continually ask God to fill you with the knowledge of his will through all the wisdom and understanding that the Spirit gives, so that you may live a life worthy of the Lord and please him in every way: bearing fruit in every good work, growing in the knowledge of God, being strengthened with all power according to his glorious might so that you may have great endurance and patience, and giving joyful thanks to the Father, who has qualified you to share in the inheritance of his holy people in the kingdom of light.

—Colossians 1:9–12

*"I have told you these things,
so that in me you may have peace.
In this world you will have trouble.
But take heart!
I have overcome the world."*

John 16:33

NEXT STEPS

The most important step you can take in the journey of healing and growth is the commitment you make to the Lord, saying *yes* to going with Him on this journey. Stay on it, regardless of how difficult it may become at different points along the way. Once your heart has determined to heal and you have engaged in the search for the resources you need to do so, the Lord is faithful to bring you the people and words you most need to encounter in each step. But you must take the step to begin.

On the Recommended Resources page, I've listed a number of books, ministries, and websites that I or others I know have found invaluable in the quest for wholeness and growth. These may be a good place for you to start. There are many thousands more out there to be found and utilized. Ask the Holy Spirit to bring you to the right situations at the right time.

I highly recommend finding a counselor who is well-equipped to deal with issues of the spirit as well as the soul and who understands the differences between the two and the nuances of their inter-connectedness. God wants to heal your whole person.

ACKNOWLEDGEMENTS

I would like to first thank my True Father. There is no one like Him and there never will be. Without Him I am nothing. Without Him, life is simply not worth living. How can words do justice to the transformation that has taken place within my soul at His hand? I look forward to spending forever attempting to express my gratitude to Him.

Secondly, I must thank the people He has sent to help me on this long journey—the oases beside a long, harsh, desert road, without whom, I would have long ago given up and let the sand bury me alive.

My sister, the inventor, the investigator, the solutioner. When I could make neither heads nor tails of my mess, you found answers that I was unlikely to find in a lifetime without you. I honor you for your sacrifice. For a time, you endured hell in isolation so that you could find the answers I needed. Curses aren't broken alone.

Magnus, I am but one of many who God has worked through you to heal. You are exceptionally good at helping people climb out of deep, dark pits to find their footing on firm ground. Your words of truth have locked doors that ought to be locked and opened bars of prisons that stood for far too long. I would not be the person I am today without you, and I thank you with all my heart for the investment of time, compassion, and kindness you have gifted me. You have taught me how to receive, and I am forever grateful.

Mia, you have been a godsend. Your ability to encourage, to understand, and to walk with me have been invaluable. I am immensely grateful for your open arms, your open ears, and most of all, your open heart.

Millie, freedom fighter, warrior, fellow curse-breaker. Thank you for broken chains, broken mindsets, and broken lies. Thank you for a sword of truth, stabbed just where I needed piercing.

This book, and my life, are the product of innumerable voices speaking the words of God through their books, sermons, podcasts, and lives lived. Many I am unlikely to meet until we cross paths in heaven. I am grateful to each of you, and I honor you for your pursuit of the ways and heart of the Lord. I look forward to celebrating with you in eternity.

RECOMMENDED RESOURCES

FOR HEALING AND GROWTH

Books:

Boundaries by Dr. Henry Cloud & Dr. John Townsend

Safe People by Dr. Henry Cloud & Dr. John Townsend

How People Grow by Dr. Henry Cloud & Dr. John Townsend

The Problem of Pain by C.S. Lewis

The Shack by William Paul Young

God Is Good by Bill Johnson

The Supernatural Power of a Transformed Mind by Bill Johnson

Unpunishable by Danny Silk

The Five Love Languages by Gary Chapman

Warring with Wisdom by Dawna De Silva

Switch on Your Brain by Dr. Caroline Leaf

Total Forgiveness by R.T. Kendall

The Supernatural Ways of Royalty by Kris Vallotton

For Women:

Captivating by John & Stasi Eldredge

Becoming Myself by Stasi Eldredge

For Men:

Wild at Heart by John Eldredge

Ministries/Websites:

Bethel's Transformation Center (SOZO, counseling, inner healing, etc.) www.betheltransformationcenter.com/

Wild at Heart (Men's inner healing) https://wildatheart.org/

Boundaries.me (Dr. Henry Cloud: healing and growth resources) https://www.boundaries.me/

BraveCo (Men's healing and growth) www.braveco.org/

AUTHOR BIO

Author Emily Benjamin is a single mother of four amazing children. In her free time, she enjoys reading, writing, studying theology, and engaging in all varieties of creative pursuits and athletic activities, especially playing soccer.

Though she has advanced degrees and has worked in ministry for a number of years, Emily considers her greatest accomplishments in life to be raising children who understand the heart of the Father for them and helping hurting people see the truth of who God is and who He has created them to be.

The greatest passion of Emily's life is to see people utterly transformed by the power and love of God. She burns for people to know and understand who God is without the structures and barriers that religion puts in their way. She longs to see people living in wholeness and freedom, carrying out the passions and callings that God has placed within them. She desires to see the church become the bride of Christ who is ready for His return.

www.ingramcontent.com/pod-product-compliance
Lightning Source LLC
Chambersburg PA
CBHW051420090426
42737CB00014B/2755